The Didjeridu:
From Arnhem Land to Internet

Acknowledgements

In an undertaking such as this there are numerous people to thank for their input and inspiration. The research has taken place over several years and continents and has profited from the kindness of informants who have put up with many questions and hopefully not too much humbug from myself and the other contributors.

Aside from the informants and contributors I especially thank Philip Hayward for giving me the opportunity to do the project and the Department of Media and Communication Studies at Macquarie University, Sydney for continuing to support Perfect Beat Publications. As well, the Aboriginal-Islander College of Music in Perth, Clarice Butkus, Noel Dyck, Mark Evans, Bernard Fernandes, David Goldsworthy, Suzanne Huebsch, the Internet participants, Kerry McKenzie, Phillip Moore, Barry Morris, Jon Stratton, the Tinleys, Janice Vercoe and the academic and support staff of the University of Newcastle (Sociology and Anthropology) all contributed either to the book itself or to the genesis of the interests and ideas that inform it. Technician Ken Scott worked diligently on many of the photographs.

* * *

This book is dedicated to my parents Lillian and Albert; my siblings Donna, Alice and Kurt; my children Erik Shah and Kyana-Lili and my grandson Kyle. May their lives be filled with music and may this book help explain what I have been doing the past few years.

The Didjeridu:
From Arnhem Land to Internet

Edited by
Karl Neuenfeldt

John Libbey

perfect beat publications

LONDON · PARIS · ROME · SYDNEY

OCm36732134

Cataloguing in Publication Data

The Didjeridu: FromArnhem Land to Internet

  Bibliography.
  Includes index.

ISBN: 1 86462 003 X (Hardback)
ISBN: 1 86462 004 8 (Paperback)

  1. Aborigines, Australian – Music.   2. Didjeridu.
  I. Neuenfeldt, Karl

  783.99

Main front and back cover photograph courtesy of George Chaloupka. The depiction of the didjeridu player is from Yuwunggayai in Arnhem Land, Northern Territory. The original image is 90 cm in height and dates from what is often referred to as the 'freshwater' period.

For further discussion of this and other Arnhem Land rock art paintings, see George Chaloupka (1993) *Journey in Time*, Sydney: Reed.

The Editors express their gratitude to John Colquohoun of Bandigan Arts & Crafts for the loan from his collection of the didjeridus photographed in the colour plate section.

Published by

John Libbey & Company Pty Ltd, Level 10, 15–17 Young Street, Sydney, NSW 2000, Australia. Telephone: +61 (0)2 9251 4099 Fax: +61 (0)2 9251 4428
e-mail: jlsydney@mpx.com.au

John Libbey & Company Ltd, 13 Smiths Yard, Summerley Street, London SW18 4HR, England;.John Libbey Eurotext Ltd, 127 Avenue de la République, 92120 Montrouge, France. John Libbey - C.I.C. s.r.l., via Lazzaro Spallanzani 11, 00161 Rome, Italy.

Printed in Australia by Gillingham Printers Pty Ltd, South Australia

Contents

About the Authors

Karl Neuenfeldt lectures in Communications and Media at Central Queensland University (Rockhampton campus) and has worked in the music industry in North and Central America and Australia variously as a performer, recording artist and producer.

Linda Barwick is an ethnomusicologist who is currently a research fellow at the University of Hong Kong. She studied central Australian women's music with Cath Ellis and is now working on the didjeridu-accompanied *wangga* and *lirrga* songs of northwest Australia.

Kev Carmody is a musician, singer-songwriter, performer and activist. In 1996 he received the Australian National Indigenous Arts Advocacy Association's award for 'Most Outstanding Contribution to Indigenous Music'.

Mick Davison is with the University of Newcastle's Aboriginal and Torres Strait Islander Education Centre. He sees himself as a 'connector', using the didjeridu to create awareness of his Goori (Aboriginal) culture.

Peter Dunbar-Hall lectures at the Conservatorium of Music, Sydney University. His PhD thesis was a study of Aboriginal rock music and he is author of several books, including *A Guide to Music Around The World*.

Philip Hayward is Head of the Department of Media and Communication Studies at Macquarie University, Sydney. He is editor of *Perfect Beat – the Pacific Journal of Research into Contemporary Music and Popular Culture* and has written and edited a number of books.

Shane Homan has played drums in various rock bands in Australia. He is currently a postgraduate student at Macquarie University, Sydney, where he is researching a doctoral thesis on the regulatory history of live music venues in New South Wales.

David Hudson is an Aboriginal musician, dancer, artist and actor. He helped establish the highly successful Tjapukai Dance Theatre, in Kuranda, Queensland, one of Australia's premier tourist attractions.

Steven Knopoff is currently an associate lecturer in ethnomusicology and music theory at the University of Adelaide and a PhD candidate at the University of Pittsburgh. He has spent 18 months studying traditional Yolngu songs in and around Yirrkala, Northern Territory.

Fiona Magowan is a lecturer in Social Anthropology at the University of Adelaide. She completed a D.Phil thesis on women's music on Elcho Island, north east Arnhem Land, at Oxford University in 1994.

Trish Sherwood lectures in the social sciences at Edith Cowan University (Bunbury campus, Western Australia) and has had a long-standing research interest in alternative communities and their belief systems.

Fred Tietjen has a private shamanic counselling practice in San Francisco. He is a collector/dealer in didjeridus and a chronicler of Aboriginal stories from both hemispheres.

Mandawuy Yunupingu is of the Yolngu people of northeastern Arnhem Land. He is an educator, political activist and musician with the group Yothu Yindi and was Australian of the Year in 1993.

YIDAKI: A Foreword

Mandawuy Yunupingu

In Australia's northeast Arnhem Land, where the so-called didjeridu originated, the instrument is known to Yolngu (Aboriginal) people as the Yidaki. The
Yidaki is deeply entrenched in Yolngu spiritual existence. It holds a special place
in the presentation of Yolngu art, music, dance and history. Its basic role in
Yolngu society is to accompany the singers, serving as a percussion instrument
as well as setting time for the rhythm of songs. Good Yidaki players are those
who start to play before they are circumcised. Once they start playing in serious
ceremonial business they build the confidence to play in public with an understanding of the rhythms of the song cycles.

The Yidaki comes from northeast Arnhem Land and was originally played only
in Australia's Top End. Yolngu understand the Yidaki has become an Australian
icon and accept that non-Yolngu people throughout the world now use it for
informal purposes and enjoyment. Be aware, however, that its origins are sacred
and secret to Yolngu men. Those stories cannot be told here, can only be shared
with initiated men. The Yidaki is a male-orientated instrument. In Yolngu society
women are forbidden to play it as its origins are sacred to men.

The tree from which Yidaki is usually cut is the Stringy Bark hollowed out by
termites. Other trees used for Yidaki manufacture include the Woollybutt and
the Bloodwoods. Yidaki players are the best people to collect them. They can be
collected all year round.

We recognise different clans' individual rhythmic processes and sounds. In
northeast Arnhem Land Yidakis tend to be long and therefore the pitch is low.
The further west we travel, the shorter the Yidaki and therefore the higher the

pitch. The Yidaki has its own language in that the tongue plays a major role in transforming air into sounds.

The Yidaki has a serious role to play in men's ceremony, but it is also used as a popular instrument that can be played for the enjoyment of women and children. Songs are distinguished between serious and fun, formal and informal. Formal songs are of a set fixed pattern and are practised formally in everyday Yolngu life. In this context it is centred on history and important events that effect Yolngu lives today and into the future. The informal context is 'fun', public enjoyment which is about contemporary Yolngu life interspersed with its formal use.

Yolngu people have long recognised the healing powers of the Yidaki. Through the provision of exercises for breathing, the Yidaki holds collective powers in the healing process. The sound transfers peaceful vibrations that penetrate the mind and create inner spiritual oneness in an individual or group. In some cases, the Yidaki is used for physical healing with the player concentrating his breath on an afflicted part of the patient's body.

Yidaki playing is a discipline encompassing art, music and history. Today it is used in the healing process between Yolngu and Balanda (Euro-Australians). Technology today accepts natural science and music, thereby opening new horizons in the study of music which combine sophisticated contemporary sounds with those of the old and draw people together in the process.

Cherish the sound, for it is the sound of Mother Earth.

Introduction

ONE INSTRUMENT, MANY VOICES

PHILIP HAYWARD AND KARL NEUENFELDT

Mandawuy Yunupingu's foreword serves to orientate or, to use a suitably musical analogy, set the tone for, this anthology of critical writings. It is appropriate that Yunupingu's is the first 'voice' encountered in this volume, since he expresses the views of the Yolngu people, one of the traditional Aboriginal communities within which the didjeridu originated. Yunupingu's foreword urges respect for the didjeridu's sacred context and use and for the dignity of Aboriginal culture. This emphasis is necessary since the didjeridu has been characterised and understood in many different ways. Consider, for instance, the following statement:

> *Its range is one note. Its sound is somewhere between a frog croaking and a horse snorting. It's called a didjeridoo and has been the primary instrument of the Australian aborigines for thousands of years. Sounds unpleasant? You bet – but then its origins are equally unpleasant. A didjeridoo is formed when termites attack the branches of a eucalyptus tree. When they've eaten away its interior, a branch is lopped off, coated with raw beeswax (presumably the termites have been cleaned out by now) and played as a wind instrument.*

> *While the didjeridoo – along with other holdovers from the Pleistocene Era like the duckbill platypus and the dingo – has evolved in Australia in almost complete isolation, the ethnic traditions of most other countries of the world have experienced the benefits of cultural cross-pollination.*

1

Their more highly developed musical languages, including unusual scales, appealing melodies and instruments made by people instead of vermin, makes these traditions more accessible and lends them an exotic beauty and charm. (Schaefer, 1990: 134)[1]

The contrast between the above quotation and Yunupingu's preface is startling. Yunupingu's text is marked by both its solemnity and its generosity in acknowledging the didjeridu's diffusion into an international context. By contrast, John Schaefer's remarks are ill-considered, ill-informed and offensive. They are marked by a contempt which is all the more startling for being written in 1990, rather than fifty or a hundred years earlier. His statement is also notable – and quotable – since it is not an obscure journalistic curio taken from a fringe right-wing publication but rather emanates from a (supposedly) more credible source. The quotation is from Schaefer's book *New Sounds – the Virgin Guide to New Music* (1990), marketed as an authoritative survey of a range of 'New Musics' (i.e. forms understood as avant garde and progressive in contrast to established classical and rock and pop conventions). The book appears complete with fulsome cover endorsements from such noted New Music figures as Philip Glass and Steve Reich.

Cross-section of a didjeridu made from a stringybark tree in New South Wales in the early 1990's, showing irregularities of the internal chamber. [Courtesy of Ken Scott, University of Newcastle.]

The contrast is between two worlds, the world of an Aboriginal musician and activist equally at home in his traditional Yirrkala community and the international music arena; and the world of a North American, metropolitan – and metro-centric – musical pundit. It is also a clash of two historical moments. Schaefer's passage precedes Yothu Yindi's breakthrough as an internationally renowned 'world music' act. His book was written at a time when the didjeridu, and Aboriginal music in general, was only of interest outside Australia to a small circle of ethnomusicologists and aficionados. Now, in the aftermath of Yothu Yindi's success, it is inconceivable that a prominent North American music writer could make such comments. The (assumed) historical purity and isolation of the instrument and its traditions are now precisely those aspects which are identified as worthy and desirable by Western enthusiasts. Indeed, the pendulum of taste has swung so far that *some* of the habitues of the North American based, and largely North American used, Dreamtime didjeridu web site and list service (didjeridu@eartha.mills.edu) are now wont to claim themselves as the guardians and truest connoisseurs of 'authentic' Aboriginal didjeridu music, even castigating Aboriginal performers who deviate from traditional styles for 'not doing justice to [their] people'.[2] (However, many of the list site habitues are more serious, politically sensitive and concerned aficionados of didjeridu music and didjeridu playing – see the discussions in Threads One and Two in this volume for evidence of this.)

At this point we should add a third perspective to orientate the project of this anthology. The quotation reproduced below is from an official report on perhaps the most sacred of (Anglo–Celtic) Australian cultural rituals, Anzac Day, the commemoration of the Australian soldiers who died in fierce combat with Turkish forces around Gallipoli in 1915, during World War One. Many commentators, both public and academic, have argued this as the foundational moment in the construction of (Anglo–Celtic) Australia's sense of nationality and national pride. It is an event commemorated and venerated by the most conservative forces in Australian society, the RSL (Returned Soldiers League) and the National Party. In 1995, the eightieth anniversary of the battle, a number of Australians (and New Zealanders) made their way to Gallipoli where Australian senator Bob McMullen lead a commemorative service.[3] David Carney later wrote that:

> *The service was very special and emotional ... An Australian backpacker, representing the crowd, touched emotions further as he read a poem ... When an apology was given for the fact that there were no bugles, a voice said 'what about a didjeridoo?' The crowd gave unanimous and enthusiastic support. A special occasion was made more special as the haunting sounds of the didjeridoo drifted out over the hills, gullies and cliff of this hallowed ground. A fitting and sombre salute to our fallen heroes.*

3

This was immediately followed by 2 minutes of silence (not a sound to be heard)[4]

The didjeridu player in question was a (white) Australian backpacker, Michael Lucas.

This incident and account offers a distinctly contemporary inflection of the Anzac myth, one in which the most quintessentially original of Aboriginal instruments can stand as an aural signifier of the (Anglo–Celtic) Australian experience of the Gallipoli landings and the germination of a distinct national identity. The irony, of course, is that Aborigines were not full citizens of Australia at the time of World War One. They were unable to vote and their culture, insofar as it was even acknowledged, was viewed within similar racist frames to those comments attributed to Schaefer above. At that time, the suggestion that the sacrifice of the sons of the newly federated Australia[5] would in future be commemorated by the sound of the didjeridu would have been unconscionable. Indeed, for much of Australia's subsequent history it would also have been unconscionable. Anzac Day 1995 took place after another, very different historical moment – and phase of national becoming – that of the Bicentennial of European settlement in 1988 and the politics and policies of national reconciliation pursued by the Keating Government in 1993–96.

The celebrations envisaged for the 1988 Bicentennial, and enacted around the shores of Sydney Harbour and on the nation's television screens, were variously influenced, inflected and subverted by a series of Aboriginal protests and cultural events which aimed to reinsert the experience, culture and rights of Aborigines into the official history of the island-continent. The momentum gained during Bicentennial Year was taken up by the Hawke Government in the late 1980s and early 1990s and accelerated under the Keating Government, when the Australian High Court's 'Mabo decision' in 1992 recognised native title in common law. However, it remains unclear if any long-term benefits for indigenous peoples will flow on from the Mabo decision given the well-organised and well-funded campaigns against indigenous land rights mounted by mining and grazing interest groups and the sympathy of the Howard Government (elected in 1996) for such initiatives. Notwithstanding the current situation, during the Keating period Aboriginal culture rapidly rose in prominence, both as a thing-in-itself and as a 'legitimate' and acceptable form of (multi-cultural) Australia. Chris Ingham (1996) has argued that far from diminishing the significance of Anzac Day, this new, inclusive, multi-cultural sensibility enhanced such anniversaries, since:

The flip-side to a growing commitment to diversity is a strong residual feeling that expresses the national imperative of a 'shared culture', where being Australian implies more than simply living here. The cul-

The didjeridu as a multicultural instrument – traditional performers Sean Choolburra (didjeridu) and Araan Fa'aso (clapsticks) (above); and Andrew Langford performing on didjeridu with singer-songwriter John Williamson (below) – both 1995.

tural nostalgia of contemporary Australia manifested in the resurgence of Anzac Day and Australia Day ... seems to express the wish that 'the Australian identity will not be so diffused ... as to lose any meaning at all.' (ibid: 18)

It was in this context and within this comparatively recent history, that the didjeridu could stand unproblematically and (apparently) so movingly, as an invocation of the spirit of Anzac.

During the early 1990s, perhaps the most visible manifestation of the arrival of Aboriginal culture within the Australian mainstream was the success of the Aboriginal rock band Yothu Yindi (who, in the spirit of the new reconciliation, included Anglo–Celtic Australian musicians in their line-up). The group released their first album in 1989 and came to prominence in 1991 with the remix of their single *Treaty*.[6] The chart success of this and subsequent releases, brought the band national attention[7] and made them a virtual icon of a (supposedly) 'new Australia'. It also gave them a springboard for international exposure, most notably in North America and Western Europe, where they introduced Aboriginal music and dance culture to the newly developed 'world music' audience.[8]

A prominent element in Yothu Yindi's music was the band's use of the didjeridu as a lead and rhythm instrument (see Knopoff, Chapter Four; and Dunbar-Hall, Chapter Five). Along with Mandawuy Yunupingu's distinctive vocals, the instrument provided the most obvious aural signifier of the band's Aboriginality. This served to promote the didjeridu as a point of identification for Aborigines from outside the areas of northern Australia where it had originally developed; to a sector of non-Aboriginal Australians willing to embrace and promote a new inflection of Australian identity; and to an international community who viewed the instrument as an important musical and/or spiritual instrument.

This anthology examines various facets of the didjeridu within this complex framework of Aboriginal, Australian and international music, culture and identity. As the title of this introduction suggests, it analyses one instrument with many voices. Some of the authors are professional performers or enthusiasts, while others are from academic backgrounds. Some authors are Aboriginal, some Euro-Australian and some European or North American. (Biographical notes are included at the beginning of this volume.) The contributions take various forms. Following Mandawuy Yunupingu's foreword, the volume combines interviews with performers, individual analyses and extracts from 'threads' – discussions about aspects of the didjeridu conducted on the Internet. We hope through this multi-vocal survey to open up discussion of the didjeridu and to encourage an understanding of the instrument as simultaneously local *and* global; as product *and* process. These facets of its cultural production and use are conceptually distinct yet inter-related in practice.

The didjeridu is now made and used by different people around the world with diverse intentions and abilities. Consequently, the didjeridu's uses and functions cannot help but change because cultures and societies, musical and otherwise, do not remain static. Like all musical instruments it is socially constructed in response to the realities of time, place and situation. Both Aborigines and non-Aborigines now utilise the didjeridu to give sound and symbol to multifaceted identities that are, in part, formed and sustained by means of music. They are actively 'making' culture in a context in which, to a large extent, practices of production and reception are undergoing transformation globally (similar to the recent marketing of Aboriginal art overseas). This making of culture is taking place in a context where boundaries are becoming increasingly porous and provisional through mass communication, the mass movements of populations and capital and the mass production of culture which circulates in the global economy.

Various chapters explore, implicitly and explicitly, the complexity of the didjeridu's cultural production and use. Mandawuy Yunupingu, Kev Carmody (Chapter One), Mick Davison (Chapter Two) and David Hudson (Chapter Three) all emphasise the manner in which the didjeridu is an important element in the maintenance and communication of Aboriginal identity, culture and pride in the multi-cultural – and/or international – contexts they perform in. Their contributions to this volume emphasise the manner in which consideration of the cultural uses and contexts of the didjeridu is not just a matter of disengaged academic inquiry but rather a very real political project which has profound implications for indigenous Australians (and those supportive of their cultural rights and integrity). While the West may chose to consider itself as an unproblematically postmodern world of endless appropriative possibilities, those outside its metrocentric core have very different perspectives. Yunupingu's foreword is important to this volume for both his account of the origins and symbolic importance of the didjeridu and his statement of the Yolngu people's 'both ways' philosophy – of seeking to preserve and assert traditional culture while engaging with the agencies, institutions and people of multi-cultural Australia.

Like Yunupingu, Carmody, Davison and Hudson all affirm the sacred origins of the didjeridu. Hudson's chapter acknowledges these aspects with regard to his work in promoting traditional Aboriginal culture. Working in a less traditional genre, Carmody discusses the influence of the didjeridu and his integration of it into contemporary performance practices. Davison's chapter more specifically identifies and discusses the role of the didjeridu in Aboriginal educational initiatives. He relates how he uses the didjeridu as an integral element in presenting Aboriginal culture to both Aboriginal and non-Aboriginal students and audiences. He provides examples of how it acts as a means of artistic expression that can serve socio-cultural and political ends by helping articulate crucial issues in Australian society.

In their respective chapters, Steven Knopoff (Chapter Four), Fiona Magowan

(Chapter Ten) and Linda Barwick (Chapter Six) draw on field work with traditional Aboriginal communities in order to discuss innovations in the use of the didjeridu. Knopoff discusses the relation between the use of the didjeridu in the traditional Yolngu clan songs and its employment in Yothu Yindi's pop/rock songs. His examination and transcriptions reveal both changes and continuities and provide insights into how distinct styles co-exist and enrich a music culture. Similarly, Magowan draws on field work in Arnhem Land, at Galiwin'ku on Elcho Island, in order to draw comparisons with the didjeridu's role(s) in Britain and Ireland. She profiles some of the most prominent composers of commercial didjeridu music in Britain and Ireland and analyses their musical innovations and personal intentions. Barwick examines the extent to which the didjeridu can be considered as a proscribed 'male' instrument in traditional Aboriginal cultures and the extent to which the gender prohibitions which are perceived to apply are subject to negotiation and contestation. Her chapter is complemented by the edited extract of an Internet discussion conducted on the list server didjeridu@eartha.mills.edu in 1995 (Thread One), addressing the issue of the gender of didjeridu players in an international context.[9]

In Chapter Five Peter Dunbar-Hall provides an overview of the use of the didjeridu in contemporary Aboriginal popular music. He outlines aspects of its traditional musical roles and geographic origins and then demonstrates how the didjeridu is being incorporated into Aboriginal popular music ensembles as an identifiably Aboriginal component. His exploration provides musicological and socio-cultural details on how new applications for the didjeridu are part of profound changes taking place in Aboriginal societies, cultures and musics. Neuenfeldt provides a different perspective on such developments in Chapter Seven by examining the advent and proliferation of the didjeridu in Central Australia, where it has become ubiquitous as an ethnographic object entangled in culture and commerce. He scrutinises its presence in and around Alice Springs and employs ethnographic data to highlight the interaction of tourists, musicians, instrument makers and retailers in the political economy of what has become an important and sizeable industry. The didjeridu is shown to be embedded in a complicated web of social organisation and relationships that are embedded, in turn, in the globalisation of culture and the commodification of indigeneity.

The remaining chapters in the anthology address aspects of the diffusion of the didjeridu into non-Aboriginal communities. Shane Homan's analysis of the career of Anglo-Celtic Australian didjeridu player Charlie McMahon in Chapter Eight complements the accounts of Aboriginal didjeridu players by detailing the manner in which non-traditional instrumentalists can pursue original approaches while still acknowledging and respecting traditional Aboriginal values. Patricia Sherwood discusses another aspect of the diffusion of the didjeridu in Chapter Nine. She investigates how 'alternative lifestylers' in Australia have appropriated and adapted the didjeridu and details their desire to construct an ideal society based on relationships that are collaborative and sustainable. Her study suggests the didjeridu's use is widespread because of its ideological affinity with alternative lifestylers' urge to reconnect with the land, with which Aborigines and, by extension, the didjeridu are thought to be intimately connected. Thread Two provides another perspective on perceptions of the authenticity and materiality of the didjeridu with its edited set of Internet exchanges around the issue of appropriate materials for didjeridu construction.

Following on from previous studies in the journal *Perfect Beat* - most notably Neuenfeldt (1993 and 1994) and Ryan (1995) – the various contributions to this anthology encourage readers to understand the didjeridu on several interconnected levels:

- as a distinctive instrument, icon and sound;

- as a nexus of social relationships;

- as a way of engaging wider theoretical issues such as appropriation, globalisation and commodification;

- and, perhaps most importantly, as a local and global product and process that will continue to develop in the soundscapes and human scapes of individuals and groups.

Overall, through and throughout its journey from Arnhem Land to the Internet and, importantly, back again, the didjeridu provides insights into the paradoxes and possibilities of musical production and use. Future issues of *Perfect Beat* will analyse other facets of the instrument's 'diaspora' and will continue to chart the instrument's progress in a range of social, cultural and musical contexts.

* * *

This anthology replaces v3 n1 of *Perfect Beat – The Pacific Journal of Research Into Contemporary Music and Popular Culture*. Further information about the journal can be obtained from the editor:
e-mail:phayward@ocs1.ocs.mq.edu.au, mail: c/o Department of Media and Communication Studies, Macquarie University, NSW 2109, Australia; or by visiting the journal's web site:
http://www.elm.mq.edu.au/pbeat/pbeat.htm

Notes

1.　There are so many factual errors and crude generalisations in this extract that it is difficult to enumerate them all here. Suffice it to say that not only does Schaefer not appear to have a musical 'ear' sufficient to identify the complexity of the didjeridu's tonal varieties; he also has little knowledge of Australia's ecology - in the Pleistocene Era or any other period.

2.　In January 1996, Sean Borman, founder and co-ordinator of the Dreamtime WWW Server, placed a posting on the Dreamtime list server (didjeridu@eartha.mills.edu) which characterised Alan Dargin's *Bloodwood* as 'disappointing' and commented that Dargin was 'not in my opinion ... doing justice to his people or the instrument' by including a (non-traditional) 'novelty' piece on the album. This lead to a major and highly volatile debate on the list server which culminated in Borman's public apology and a statement of his intention to resign.

3.   After speaking at an official ceremony, to which the travellers were not admitted, McMullen was persuaded to hold a second impromptu service. Carney's description refers to this alone.

4.   David Carney, 'Epilogue - We still remember them ...', in (unattributed, unpaginated, undated) commemorative booklet *The People's Ceremony - Lone Pine 25 April 1995* compiled for Senator Bob McMullen (and – presumably – printed by his office).

5.   Australia only became federated in 1901.

6.   Whereas the first version failed to chart, the 'Filthy Lucre' remix was a major hit.

7.   For further discussion of the cultural politics of Yothu Yindi's success and promotion in Australia see Hayward (1993) and Nicol (1993).

8.   See Feld (1994) for further discussion.

9.   See the introduction to Thread One for further details about the context of the debate.

Bibliography

Feld S. (1994) 'From Schizophonia to Schismogenesis: On the Discourses and Commodification Processes of "World Music" and "World Beat"', in Feld S. and Keil C. *Music Grooves*, Chicago: University of Chicago Press.

Hayward P. (1993) 'Safe, Exotic and Somewhere Else – Yothu Yindi, *Treaty* and the Mediation of Aboriginality', *Perfect Beat* v1 n2, January.

Ingham C. (1996) 'Creative Clever Nation Anzac Vision Thing', *Arena* n23, June–July.

Neuenfeldt K. (1993) 'The Didjeridu and the Overdub – Technologising and Transposing Aural Images of Aboriginality', *Perfect Beat* v1 n2, January.

Neuenfeldt K. (1994) 'The Essentialistic, The Exotic, The Equivocal and The Absurd – The Cultural Production and Use of the Didjeridu in World Music', *Perfect Beat* v2 n1, July.

Nicol L. (1993) 'Custom, Culture and Collaboration – The Production of Yothu Yindi's *Treaty* Videos', *Perfect Beat* v1 n2, January.

Ryan R. (1995) 'Gnarnayarrahe Waitairie, *Claim* and *Pundulumura*', *Perfect Beat* v2 n2, January.

Schaefer J. (1990) *New Sounds – the Virgin Guide to New Music*, London: Virgin.

Chapter One

ANCIENT VOICE – CONTEMPORARY EXPRESSION

The Didjeridu (Yidaki) and the Promotion of Aboriginal Rights

KEV CARMODY with Karl Neuenfeldt

K ev Carmody is an Aboriginal musician, social activist and self-confessed 'propagandist' for indigenous peoples in Australia and elsewhere.[1] He has recorded four albums (see Discography) and performed extensively nationally and internationally. His artistry is firmly rooted in the oral tradition and he was originally characterised as being within the Dylanesque tradition of 'protest' singer-songwriters. However, Carmody has branched out to present his insightful and forceful lyrics in an eclectic range of musical styles. He uses the didjeridu in performance and recording.

Carmody was born in Queensland and grew up on a cattle station. Like many Aboriginal children of his generation, he was taken from his family and placed in an institution that he now considers to have been more of an orphanage than a school. He worked as a general labourer for seventeen years before returning to formal education and obtaining a BA (Dip.Ed.). He has had a long-standing commitment to issues of social justice that impact on indigenous communities (such as the over-representation of Aborigines in the prison system and the wants and needs of street kids and the protection of the environment). He is now well

Kev Carmody (1995).

known and regarded within Australian popular music and has been the subject of magazine, newspaper and academic articles (see, for instance Johnson, 1993) and a television documentary, *From Little Things Big Things Grow*.[2] The title is taken from a song he wrote with non-indigenous singer-songwriter Paul Kelly about an Aboriginal protest to obtain fair wages in the pastoral industry. The song won an Australian Country music Golden Guitar Award in 1994 as Heritage Song of the Year. This is ironic given that Australian Country music's core non-indigenous constituency tends to oppose Aboriginal aspirations, especially the land rights that are integral to indigenous peoples' heritage. Carmody says the song may not really qualify as a Country song, but 'the award illustrates not only the easing of conservative values of the country and western audience, but the broadening of definitions and categories of music everywhere' (cited in Dawes, 1994: 24). The Heritage Song of the Year Award illustrates that Kev Carmody's songs are not restricted to 'protest', they are much more. They are identity narratives for the nation, for both indigenous and non-indigenous Australians and his use of the didjeridu helps to narrate that identity. (*Karl Neuenfeldt*)

***

KC: My mother's people are the Lama-Lama people from Cape York Peninsula of northern Queensland, south of Coen, north of Laura and inland from Cooktown. My grandfather was born at Breeza Plains right in the middle of that country. The different Dreamings run right through that whole area. There are different songs for each and they're all interconnected. Its just amazing how Moon Dreaming overlaps with Dingo Dreaming, like the cycle of the moon and the howl of a dingo and runs right through Brolga Dreaming right up to Windsong Dreaming and so on. The sound of the didjeridu is just a wonderful way of carrying and expressing a musical culture.

KN: *What are your earliest memories of didjeridu and can you translate that to performance?*

KC: One of my first memories was hearing it around the camp fire. The night food had been cooked, it'd been eaten, people were relaxed. The flame of the fire had gone down and you've got a big bed of coals and you look at those coals and you can see the infinity of existence in that fire. You've got the light that it throws around amongst the trees and you've got the night sky above you. You've got the whole surreal scenario of existence. Then you will hear the clap-sticks and you will hear the drone of the didj and then you will see the dust of the dance.

It's just something that's so spiritual [and] empowering and enlightening that it'd virtually be impossible to replicate on a stage. But that's how I remember that spiritual affinity with that sound and the magical spiritual feeling of being around the camp fire. The way things move, the leaves, the reflection of light, the moon and the stars and the people. It's just a magical thing. I mean, it's a spiritual experience. You don't have to go to a cathedral to have a priest out front to show you what spirituality is. In fact, I don't think they've got it.

KN: *How did you learn to play the didjeridu?*

KC: It was an old great uncle of mine that taught me didjeridu and what he taught me represented a series of songlines. So as you're playing it, you're going on a journey with the music in your own mind. Depending on the night, the time, wherever the moon is, or your surrounds, you will play it differently. The actual mechanics of playing doesn't take too long to learn but the background behind the instrument is what [he] taught me. The didjeridu's just a massive instrument and I never sit down with it without having a sense of awe.

KN: *Was the didjeridu something that was around all the time when you were a kid?*

KC: It was a constant subject of conversation I suppose because really it was part of living life for my old grandfather. And then when my old great uncle was talking about the didj I connected those things that my old grandfather told me into the playing of the didj. It sounds really simplistic and child-like I suppose but my old great uncle taught me that you take the air from the mother earth, put it into your lungs, blow down that hollow tube and you make a sound. But a little bit of your spirit goes out with that mother earth. So in that sense the didj's got a sacredness about it. When you're making that sound it's a very special thing that you're doing and that was impressed on me.

KN: *How do you usually use the didjeridu in performance? Do you use it to pace the sets or as a change from the intense and image-packed content of your lyrics?*

KC: Well, didj certainly is a change from the lyric content. It's just an amazing reaction you get. I've played it before up to two and a half thousand people in a concert hall solo and there's just this amazing silence afterwards, a real spiritual infinity with the universe after you finish. It's like such an intense musical journey for three to four minutes that people and myself just sit there stunned at what this instrument represents.

The didjeridu's such a complicated instrument. The majority of people only hear it as a rock percussive instrument but there are three things that happen when you blow it. [First] is the pitch, which is the drone note. [Second] you can play any rhythm you like through it. And the [third] thing that happens is you can pitch your voice to any interval, which busts up the western tone scale like nothing. Those three things combined make it an extremely complicated instrument.

KN: *What about your use of didjeridu in a recording context? How do you think of it from the point of view of a producer in the more controlled environment of a recording studio?*

KC: It certainly loses something in the studio. I mean the didj loses a hell of a lot really, it becomes limited once you record it. I've rarely ever played it myself [on recordings], I've always got other players in to play. John Lacey was the player [on the *Bloodlines* album (1993)]. He could turn cartwheels as far as technique goes. But it's that spiritual feel you've got to get into it. As the old man said to me, you've got to blow it as lightly as you can till there's just hardly any breath coming out of ya and you're still making sound. He said that's where it really counts, that real gentleness of the didj.

14

What we did with John was we put a microphone down at the end of the tube. But I thought it would be interesting just to see the rhythmic variation you can get if we put a microphone up at his nose, so you can get the breathing, that's rhythm too. Breath is just as important as the sound coming out of the end. That's what the old fellow told me. And it's just amazing the difference that songs took on by recording the sound of the nose breathing in the air. It just made a completely different textural content to the music, which was exciting. I'd like to do that on stage myself but it's usually too difficult. I mean, it's not complicated but it looks too over-blown on stage. I just like the microphone on the floor so I can sit and make it seem as simple as anything and play this complicated, magical sound.

KN: *So in the context of performance it adds a different dimension to what you're presenting as far as your perspective on music or Aboriginality or politics?*

KC: Oh for sure, for sure. I think quite a good way to start it all is to just breathe and pick up that sound of the human breath through this hollow instrument and then start to blow. Because it's your breath from the earth that's going to produce the sound. It's just a good little prelude I think before you start.

KN: *Given your involvement in Australian politics could you comment on how the didjeridu has moved into the political iconography and symbolism of pan-Aboriginality. Has it superseded the boomerang or 'black fellas-in-loin-cloths-leaning-on-spears' type of images?*

KC: Well, it has certainly changed. People relate to symbols. It's just like stop signs, give way signs, or coloured lights. Certainly the didj has moved into that area of representation. It's something that's unique to this country and certainly they use it. How should I say it, things get subsumed in some ways.

KN: *What about the issue of appropriation in that the didjeridu is being used globally by non-Aboriginal people and in Australia by Aboriginal people who may or may not have had it as part of their traditional musical culture?*

KC: Well I suppose it's just like me picking up a cello or any instrument I play, like a guitar or banjo. There's a piece of me goes into that playing. And all my values, background, philosophy, my heritage. I'll play the cello a lot different to a symphony orchestra player same as with a guitar or didj. Non-Aboriginal people *can* play it. Even urban blackfellas will play it different to traditional Aboriginal people. It's just like you doing an assignment at university. It's going to be different to mine because our values, our backgrounds are completely different. So in that sense there's an indigenous stamp on it from even the urban Aborigines as opposed to the non-Aboriginal people. To [the colonisers] it's just sound, it's just another instrument. But to us Aborigines, I suppose it's a spiritual expression in many different forms.

KN: *Have you encountered what you would consider to be inappropriate use or misappropriation in your travels in Europe or North America?*

KC: I encountered that in the Netherlands. We were doing a gig and all of a sudden after we had finished six of these males jumped up on stage with all sorts of instruments. The instruments were hollow tubes but they weren't wood from this country so I could hear all these different sounds with the didj. They were blowing and making all the noises and stuff but there was just no grounding, there was no earthing of the sound. It was just sound. It was just like switching on a CD. Then they invited me to get up and play. And I thought 'These fellas want some stamp of authenticity'. So I got up and played with them. It was almost chaotic, it was this massive bloody sound of six didjs playing but there was no anchoring. You could hear them trying to listen to what I was doing and pull it back because it has got to be earthed. It has got to have some sense of geographic place to make sense. To me that really exemplified what happens once they move away from the Dreaming place, the geographic place. I can travel all around the world but I've still got the sense of place when I play the didj. To me they were all making good didj noises but there was no spiritual affinity and anchoring of where it should be.

KN: *In your own life-time you've seen the didjeridu go from a local instrument, to an Australian national pan-Aboriginal instrument, to a global instrument. What are your observations on this process, which in many ways is an incredible journey in a short time for any musical instrument?*

KC: When I see it played in North America or Europe it's usually by people who are striving to find a new sense of spiritual identity. You'll mostly find it in the alternative areas, which goes across all classes by the way. It's like religion has so alienated so many people [that] they're looking for the spiritual affinity that we have with this country. I think that's what they're trying to do in some ways, or trying to express with the instrument, to discover the old spirituality which the didjeridu represents.

KN: *What do you feel about the inclusion of didjeridu in Aboriginal pop music in groups such as Warumpi Band, Coloured Stone, Yothu Yindi, Blek Bela Mujik, etc? Has it become the main sonic symbol of Aboriginality?*

KC: For sure, that's why it stands out so much. But again I look at it this way: it's that spiritual context being put into a modern medium. It's the ancientness of the instrument and what it represents spiritually being put into mainstream music. That's why it's so unique.

KN: *Why do you use didjeridu solo in performance?*

KC: Playing it solo anchors it back to what I knew it [to be], that's why it has such a massive impact. I think it's time for us to reclaim it back to that context again. Just one fellow on stage with it, no clap sticks, nothing. It has just gone everywhere [globally], as we've been discussing and I think once people actually see it in that [solo] context and then with the dance, with the clap-sticks and the whole ceremonial context, the impact's phenomenal. But this is one tiny way to do it, just do it solo and reclaim the didjeridu back. It's like what we [indigenous peoples] are doing now on [days such as today], Invasion Day [also known as Australia Day – which commemorates for European Australians the arrival of the First Fleet]. What we're doing playing for the Survival Concert [at the Aboriginal community at La Perouse south of Sydney] is reclaiming back that cultural heritage through music. And I think we can just turn it back the other way and say look at the power of the didjeridu as an instrument: spiritual power.

KN: *Given the increasing popularity of indigenous music and musicians, do you see the arts in general and music in particular, as one way for colonisers in a sense to re-humanise indigenous people that they had to dehumanise in order to rationalise full-scale ethnocide and genocide?*

KC: I don't ever feel that I was ever dehumanised. The oppression that I lived through and am still living through in some ways, it just made me feel that the colonisers were dehumanised. They were the inhumans. They were the spiritual paupers and I always felt a sadness for a people and a system that is inhuman. I never felt that dehumanised at all. I just felt, gee we've got a long, long hard haul here to rehumanise these [colonising] people. It wasn't me [who colonised]!

KN: *How do you approach performance, both in your presentation of songs and the didjeridu?*

KC: I found out real early on, twenty or thirty year ago, [that] unless you can bridge that six foot between the microphone stand and the first row [of an audience] you might as well not be there. That's why I talk between the songs. I cannot divorce story-telling from song, or from dance, or from art. And what I found in the music industry is that there's two ways of doing it: one is the Nuremburg Rally concept which is to overpower the audience with your ego, your music, your new style. That is, two hundred stacks of Marshall amplifiers and that whole music business that we've seen happen. The other way that I've found, that I try to utilise, is to empower the audience to be part of the performance so it becomes a two-way thing. And then, in a broad sense, one performance. They're part of it. They're brought into it. They're not outsiders that you're jamming your stuff down their neck, they're with you. They may disagree. They may look at it from different view points, but it's that empowering of both the performer and the audience that I feel people go away with [from my performances].

KN: *What do you see as possible roles for the use of the didjeridu in school curriculums?*

KC: When they first put me in school when I was ten year old, I learnt very quickly the difference between education, which is the system's propaganda for an economic outcome, [and learning]. Education was a real control mechanism upon the intellect. Learning was something different. Up until I was ten years old, to me learning [was] the fostering of the curiosity of the imagination of the human intellect. 360 degree thinking, everything was relevant, that was really fostered. If you go and play [didj] to young children like the primary school mob, you really hit the button because their intellects haven't been channelled. You go and play it to the third year graduates at university, the intellect's already been consolidated into the State's education system. I think [the didj and Aboriginal music] has a tremendous role to play while the intellect hasn't been cemented. I'd love to work in that area with not only the didj but with a heap of different things because we certainly can change people's awareness with it. We can't change their mentality, that's Hitler's way of doing it or Pol Pot's or bloody capitalism's, but at least we can make them aware. If we leave them to make up their own mind, in the long term, we could get a change I'm sure.

KN: *How do you feel about the use of Aboriginal popular music in schools? Have some of your own recordings been included in curriculum or used for teaching purposes?*

KC: We never sell many records, fair dinkum. Five thousand is the most we've ever sold with an album, but the amount of requests we get from high school students, from primary school students, from academics, from professors [is considerable]. To me, that's the positive part of the whole thing. I just feel really optimistic, in the long term of maybe three hundred years time, that the little bits that we're starting off now reclaiming of the culture ourselves and then transmitting it to the wider population [will have an effect]. The didj is one way, one way we can at least start.

KN: *Do you think it is possible to separate the didjeridu as entertainment, empowerment or education?*

KC: Just speaking personally, I can't [separate them]. That's why I always try to get the lighting person on stage to put all the lights out or right down [when I play didjeridu]. [As if to say] 'This is the spiritual expression we're gonna do and it's special. It's not jangling on a guitar'. I'm trying to replicate that feel [of how I first heard the didjeridu] in a minuscule way and then I start to play and just try to get a tiny fraction of that [spirituality] to empower the audience.

KN: *So are you entertaining, empowering and educating all at the same time?*

KC: It's not me, it's the old people educating me. I'm just a vehicle through which that expression comes.

Notes

1. In a survey of politicised artists with national and international impact, Lipsitz (1994) includes Carmody along with Thomas Mapfumo of Zimbabwe, Alpha Blondy of Ivory Coast, Johnny Clegg of South Africa and Gilles Vigneault of Quebecois Canada. Lipsitz suggests the cultural production of their music: 'enables people to rehearse identities, stances and social relations not yet permissible in politics' (137).

2. The incident recounted in the song is the 1966 'strike' of the Gurindji people, led by Vincent

Lingiarri, on a pastoral holding of a multinational owner, Lord Vestey. It was an important minor event, along with the 1979 failed Yolngu Arnhem Land land rights claim, that contributed indirectly to a major event: the 1992 Australian High Court *Native Title in Common Law* decision that lead to the 'Mabo' legislation.

Bibliography

Dawes S. (1994) 'Review of Triple J *Earthcore* Compilation Album', *X-Press*, n401 Perth, Australia.

Johnson R. (1993) 'Looking Out: An Interview with Kev Carmody', *Perfect Beat* v1 n2 January.

Lipsitz G. (1994) *Dangerous Crossroads: Popular Music, Postmodernism and the Poetics of Place*, London: Verso.

Discography

Kev Carmody *Pillars of Society*, Larrikin, 1990.

Kev Carmody *Eulogy (For a Black Person)*, Larrikin, 1991.

Kev Carmody *Bloodlines*, Larrikin, 1993.

Kev Carmody *Images and Illusions*, Larrikin, 1995.

Chapter Two

EDUCATION, EMPOWERMENT AND ENTERTAINMENT

An Aboriginal Perspective on the Didjeridu

MICK DAVISON with Karl Neuenfeldt

Mick Davison is the Aboriginal and Torres Strait Islander Students' Cultural Support Officer at the University of Newcastle, New South Wales, Australia. He works in the Wollotuka Centre, which caters to the educational and personal needs of Aboriginal and Torres Strait Islander students. Davison is a Koori from New South Wales. His job is multi-faceted. He helps students with accommodation, finances, studying and tutoring and whatever other difficulties may arise. Davison's extensive and innovative use of the didjeridu is a unique aspect of his teaching philosophy which blends education, empowerment and entertainment.

Recently there has been a concerted effort on the part of universities and technical schools across Australia to encourage indigenous students to get involved in tertiary education. This current trend needs to be appreciated in the historical context of the long-running and active discouragement by governments and religious institutions of indigenous students gaining all but the most basic education. Especially during the 'Assimilation Era', which lasted until at least the 1960s, most indigenous people were thought to be incapable of being educated beyond a minimal level (and then only as domestic or manual labourers). Due to the policy of taking children away from their families and fostering

Mick Davison (left) performing with school students (1995).

or institutionalising them and the policy in some states at least, of allowing school principals to exclude Aboriginal pupils without a formal reason, many indigenous children received insufficient or intermittent formal education and were rarely encouraged to develop themselves academically. It is fair to say that many indigenous students' experience of Western education and its institutions has been, and frequently continues to be, negative.

Retention rates for indigenous students in secondary schools are very low and many enter tertiary education as mature students. The findings of the Royal Commission into Aboriginal Deaths in Custody (Tickner *et al.* 1992) recognised that mainstream education, often lacking cultural suitability, has been a major contributor to the disadvantage experienced by many indigenous people in that 'school based education systems have been either unable or unwilling to accommodate many of the values, attitudes, codes and institutions of Aboriginal and Torres Strait Islander people in Australian society'. (40) The advent of supportive centres such as Wollutuka, in-depth overviews such as the National Review of Education for Aboriginal and Torres Strait Islander Peoples (1994) and the work of committed educators such as Davison are helping address not only the under-representation of indigenous students in tertiary education but also the previous almost total lack of presence of indigenous peoples or their perspectives in mainstream educational materials and curricula at all levels.

For both Aboriginal and non-Aboriginal students, exposure to or participation in Aboriginal music per se was almost non-existent prior to the 1990s. A notable exception is the work of Cath Ellis whose pioneering book *Aboriginal Music, Education for Living: Cross Cultural Experiences from South Australia* (1985) provides useful insights and rationales for the inclusion of music as a vehicle for wider educational and socio-cultural agenda. Ellis advances an opinion that provides a wider context for the use of the didjeridu:

> *In the process of the education of the total person which occurs through the use of music, the student may learn relatively little about music (although this is not necessarily so). But he inevitably gains a great deal of experience in reconciling and rising above contradictions both within himself and in his relations with others.*(2)

This quote epitomises Davison's efforts to educate, empower and entertain the whole person, be they Aboriginal or non-Aboriginal, by means of the didjeridu. (*Karl Neuenfeldt*)

KN: *How would you describe your job and what do you try to do?*

MD: I go out into the community promoting not just Wollotuka but Aboriginal Education and encouraging young Aboriginal men and women into either university or TAFE College [Tertiary and Further Education] or [some other type of] higher education. I try and get them to aim at that level and then to create the awareness that if they want to take part in the future of the country they've got to start somewhere with education. It doesn't necessarily have to be higher education, it can be starting off in courses you do in [a government sponsored training program like] 'Skillshare' and then once you get your confidence you go on from that.

KN: *How do you use Aboriginal music in education and what is your intended end result?*

MD: All I use is the didjeridu ... usually at the end [of a lecture]. I'll go into a school and talk about whatever the issues are they want me to talk about. For example, if I was talking to the history students I would speak on that perspective. But I usually try and leave the last fifteen to twenty minutes to actually introduce the didjeridu and do a meditation type thing and demystify it. I show how we get all the sounds, then get people to listen to it with their eyes closed. Then I try and get them to capture the images that they see as well as the feelings. And they really can't because it's different every time, but it's great letting them know that they can't capture it.

I think the end result [is] I use the didjeridu to create an awareness with non-indigenous people and Aboriginal people as well, because a lot of Aboriginal people don't know a lot of our history because of being taken away when they were kids. The ultimate aim … is to let those people walk away thinking about Aboriginal issues.

KN: *How long have you been playing the didjeridu and over the course of a year, how many performances of different types have you done?*

MD: I've been playing didjeridu the last ten years or thereabouts. I've done most of the schools in the Hunter region of New South Wales. There's a fair few hundred of high schools, primary schools and pre-schools. A rough figure would probably be between two hundred to five hundred schools in the last ten years. That's just the schools and then outside of that I've played at flag-raising ceremonies, weddings and funerals and other things. Sometimes friends call me over and I take my didj with me. The next minute I'm playing it at their place for ten or twenty minutes. Then the next night I might be doing something like recording and there's another hour or so there. So, in the last ten years I've been averaging at least three to four hours a week, which seems a lot but when you're enjoying it you don't really worry about it. If I was told that I had to play it four hours a week, then I probably wouldn't do it!

KN: *Do you think the didjeridu can be an effective tool in teaching students about Aboriginal issues?*

MD: I think [it can] because what I'm doing with the didjeridu at the moment is using it to back up what I'm saying. I always talk about Aboriginal issues [and] look at the education side of it and the housing and employment [side] … But the ultimate thing is I always mention the culture and the spirituality side. That's why I finish off with the didjeridu. That way people have heard all of the issues, they've heard all about what had happened on both the black history and the white history side. When I finish it with the didjeridu it seems to put it all into context. They're saying, 'Well O.K., yeah, now we know where these people are coming from. Now we know how they feel about the land and how they were connected to that type of religion with the land'. I think that's where the didjeridu helps me, it actually finishes off and backs up what I've just said for the first hour or forty minutes in the lecture.

I don't think that when I went out and just talked about Aboriginal issues [it was as effective] … [But] when the didjeridu came along, it just seemed to enhance it and make it stick in people's minds. What the image I'm getting is that I talk about Aboriginal issues … and then when I play the didjeridu that seems to stamp it in people's minds.

Somewhere they might be talking with their friends, they might be in a lecture or they might be doing an assignment or whatever. Then the image I get of them is saying, 'Oh yeah, Mick mentioned something about that' and then they'll think of it. And they'll say 'Righteo, the didjeridu', zero in on the sound and then pick out what happened in the lecture. So it's sort of like a reminder. It's like replaying the answer-phone message on the telephone machine. They zero in on that sound and then when they listen to that sound they say 'Oh, that's right, he mentioned this'. So I can see it as a good reminder.

KN: *Does the didjeridu provide a special kind of sonic association?*

MD: Yeah, that's right. And that's a whole new field now for me to get into. It's interesting because I'm not seeing where it's heading to [when I use it] but it's good experiencing it as well as the people that I'm talking to. Because when I imagine the sound in my mind, it'll take and I'll say 'Oh, that's right, I can remember talking to this group' and I did this particular sound and whatever. So [sonic association is also] actually helping me remember certain things that I feel are important.

KN: *Have you had experiences with other indigenous cultures?*

MD: ... I've been looking at other different cultures, having a few experiences with them. In 1993 at Singleton [New South Wales] in the Year of the Indigenous People I actually played the didj with two [North] American [Native] Indian women. I had always wanted to play the didj with the tom-tom drums from North American Indians ... [The music] was just part of the whole day, there was all groups there. There were Maori, Aboriginals and Native Indians ... [The Native Indians] came over and said, 'Would you mind playing the didjeridu with us'?. They started to play the tom-tom drums and then [one of the women] started singing ... all about the land ...

I asked the [Native Indians] what is the significance. I said, 'Look, you've probably been asked this question a million times the same as I've been asked the same question about the didj a lot of times'. She said the tom-tom drum was the heartbeat of the earth, of our mother, the earth. I thought, right and that set me off on a whole new trail ... So I'm looking at the central part of all indigenous cultures and their responsibilities and I'm now looking at the earth like a big brain. I'm looking at how indigenous people now through their music are actually part of looking after the whole planet ...

KN: *So in a sense the didjeridu goes beyond being just a musical instrument?*

MD: The didj is now teaching me to look at all issues, environmental issues and all that spirituality. It's actually taking me there through the meditations ... It's like a teacher for me and that's the good thing I like about it. Rather than just to grab it and play it and get whatever I can out of it, what I'm doing is letting it take me to all these different places ... What didj is doing for me personally is taking me through a lot of doors. I'll have an experience with it and then out the next door and then do something else with it. So, for me I'm looking at didj as a really good teacher. I don't know if anybody is looking at it that way. As I experience a lot of things with it, that's what I talk about, this is how it's affected me.

KN: *So it has several complementary roles?*

MD: Yeah, there's a good little mutual thing there. I don't overpower it, it doesn't overpower me to a certain extent. We're riding along pretty good together … Ninety nine per cent of the time the didj is with me, just in the back of the car or strapped on my back. If people don't actually ask for it, I don't take it [but] then when I turn up without it the first thing they ask is for the didj! So it's like we're pretty inseparable at the moment. A lot of people say, 'What would you do without the didj'? And then I say, 'Well, what would the didj do without me'?

I thought, well I got to look at what's happening with the didj and myself and so now it's [important] to try and document [how I use it] … Now what's happening is that there are some students at the university here at Newcastle … doing their honours [degrees] and a few of them are looking at using me [as an informant]. So I thought, gee what a great way to get it documented because I haven't got time to do it. So they're going to follow me out around all over the place, so in a way I'm actually getting something from the didj.

The didj is saying, 'Well, look Mick you haven't got time to sit down and do all this because while you're sitting down trying to put it on computer and write it, you're not out here'. That's basically what it's saying. Suddenly students are just coming in the door and getting me to write a letter of recommendation to their supervisors about how their involvement in looking at me with education and the didjeridu will create better relationships between Aboriginal and non-Aboriginal people and all that sort of thing. So that's one [aspect of education] that's actually being documented through the didj and me.

KN: *When you are teaching, what do you feel is important for the students to understand and how does the didjeridu help you achieve that?*

MD: Well basically with the didj I don't ever prepare a lecture before I go in. Because [with] the didjeridu I don't actually know what I'm going to play until I actually play it. I never prepare it because if I sit down and I look at it a night or two before, that's the thoughts for those nights … [For example, if] I'm going to prepare a lecture … and I'm going to say this and this [but] then when I get into the room there's non-Aboriginal students there [or] 80 per cent could be women or men. So I've got to direct it to the minority group as well, the 20 per cent of women or men there. So what I've written just two nights ago doesn't apply.

So now with the didjeridu it's actually helping me lecture because the first thing I do is [look at the audience and] think, 'O.K. there's 80 per cent of men here and 20 per cent women so I've got to remind the men that there are women here and they're involved in this as well. [Or] 60 per cent of this audience is over-forty or under-forty so that I've got to mention something along those lines'. While I'm there I look around the room and formulate what I'm going to say and then if it's a sociology group I go along that line, if it's a history group I go along that line.

Before I go in, if I've nothing up here in the brain that I've mentally prepared to a certain extent, what I'll do is just find a space somewhere and play the didj for about four or five minutes. I do a little bit of meditation, clear all the rubbish out of the brain and then I'm focused. So when I go in I can say I'm ready to go … It's like having a filing cabinet. I'll say, right, this group is over this particular age so I'll go to this little drawer and draw this out, my experiences at that particular age or whatever. Then women's issues … I say, right, my grandmother comes into play then and my mother and what happened [with them]. So suddenly the didjeridu is actually starting to help me to lecture without any fear … It's educating me to articulate the whole lot. I'm still working on how it does that.

KN: *What about when a school is fifty/fifty Aboriginal and non-Aboriginal students? How do you approach that, given that, in some of the communities there are problematic racial relations?*

MD: The way I approach that is I still basically talk about Aboriginal education and history and all that type of thing but I always [say] that Aboriginal kids have one advantage over the non-Aboriginal kids. That advantage is Aboriginal kids know the non-Aboriginal history. I knew where [migrants] come from, why, how and when, [such as the voyages of] Captain Cook and that it was overcrowded in England [and the government wanted to get rid of 'criminals'] … That's the advantage we had over the non-Aboriginal kids, we knew their history but the non-Aboriginal kids don't know about the black history.

That's where I say, 'Well, look, this is why I'm here today. I'm talking to the Aboriginal kids as well but the non-Aboriginal kids after today will be able to go home and teach their parents about Aboriginal history'. So I'll talk about personal type things with me or other stories that I've heard in my travels to give them both a knowledge and background to take home with and argue with. Whether it's with their parents or whether it's with their friends.

I'm saying the same thing [to Aborigines and non-Aborigines] except acknow-ledging that as an Aboriginal person I value the non-Aboriginal people in this room. And that's what I say. I say, the reason I value you people is because you are going to help rewrite the books. You're going to help get rid of all the prejudicial language that was in those books where your parents got their prejudices from. So, as an Aboriginal person, you people are very important to me as non-Aboriginal people because you're the ones that are going to help break down all the prejudices over the years and you're going to rewrite the history books and you're going to help in breaking down a lot of the barriers.

KN: *Do you have any specific strategies you use when you go into a school that is all Aboriginal students?*

MD: It is really interesting to experience ninety per cent of the kids being Aboriginal in a school. Because when I grew up, we were lucky to make up two or three per cent. So it was interesting going out to places like Bourke, Briwarrina and Walgett [in western New South Wales] and actually speak to the kids about us, Aboriginal people.

I approached it in this way. I'd look at the kids and I'd say, well O.K., I'm going to get these kids, who were sort of from the Outback, to know a little bit about [the outside world]. They always looked to the closest bigger town and to them it was probably like us going to New York for the first time. It is very overwhelming ... I think it's like the Paul Hogan movie, *Crocodile Dundee* [where] he's walking up the main street saying g'day to everyone. That's the image they have of the nearest big town. So when I go to the schools, I basically give them that image and say, well O.K., this is what's out there, but don't forget there are Aboriginal people like me out there too. So make sure you get in contact with us to make sure we can help you through hurdles that you have to jump to get to wherever you want to get to.

I basically give them the history of how to survive in an urban situation. And then I always say to them, 'Why do you want to live out here, there's nothing out here'? And then they tell me about how they survive and what's out here. They'll talk about, 'Oh we've got fishing and we can go hunting'. And I thought that's a good stress-free life. I always let them know that they're just as important as far as what they do, as what we do. So it's mentally preparing them if they want to get something out here [in the urban world], a degree or a diploma. I try to prepare them for what's out here. I try to give them role models, like [politician, bureaucrat and activist] Charlie Perkins, myself and Aboriginal people who have become lawyers like Paul Coe, Michael Mansell and other [Aboriginal] people around the country. I always say to them, 'These people have come from areas like this, gone into the cities or wherever, got their bits of paper, got used to the system and now they're helping Aboriginal people'. And if [the students] ever get into any hassles, they can ring us up and say, 'Hey look, I'm thinking about chucking my job in, I'm thinking about running away' ... Then we can say, 'Hey look, what you're doing is important, I know it's important'. We're always encouraging each other. I've told them that's how you can survive out here. It's just a matter of picking the phone up and having a yarn.

KN: *So how does the didjeridu help present that knowledge?*

MD: For me now it's like a calling card, I suppose. I'll come into the place, have a bit of a yarn, [and] give them a really incredible experience with the didj as far as the mental pictures and the feelings and [information]. I think that's giving people a little bit of a spiritual strength somewhere along the line. So when they get into a situation or a hassle, then they can go and retreat somewhere into a corner and close their eyes and basically re-live the sound [of the didjeridu]. You can do it mentally and it can relax you. I think that's one of the ultimate reasons why I try and use the didj as much as I can in everything I do because that's connecting them back to that strength.

KN: *Of your three kinds of uses for Aboriginal music (education, empowerment and entertainment), which one is most important?*

MD: I think they're all pretty well wrapped up together … They'd all probably get thirty three and a third per cent each because to me they're all important … To me they're three equal things happening all the time.

KN: *Can you sum up what the impact of the didjeridu as education, empowerment and entertainment might be?*

MD: I think the didj is doing two things. It's taking people to the past … and [it's] bringing us to the future as well, because we've still got to maintain some of that as well. So for me, it's re-connecting people with our Aboriginal culture, which is what people thought we lost but we haven't really. I mean, I'm reconnecting them with it and giving people a new appreciation of it through the didj. They're really saying, 'Well, gee, these Aboriginal people had something there and it's affecting me now, today, this year, this minute'. For me it's giving the person today that connection with forty thousand, sixty thousand years of history. That's an amazing thing for the person to actually just experience that connection. [Or] just even to think about it. Because what [the didjeridu is] saying is that it's not forty thousand, sixty thousand years old. What happened then can actually be in the future. And if we want that type of thing in the future, we've got to think about it now.

Bibliography

Ellis C. (1985) *Aboriginal Music, Education for Living: Cross Cultural Experiences from South Australia*, St. Lucia: University of Queensland Press.

National Review of Education for Aboriginal and Torres Strait Islander People (1994), Canberra: Australian Government Service.

Tickner, R *et al.* (1992) *Aboriginal Deaths in Custody: Overview of the Responses by Governments to the Royal Commission*. Canberra: Australian Government Printing Service.

Chapter Three

THE DIDJERIDU – A PORTAL TO CULTURE

DAVID HUDSON with Fred Tietjen

David Hudson is an Aboriginal musician, dancer, painter, story-teller, documentary film-maker and actor. Born on Cape York Peninsula, in northern Queensland, Hudson grew up during the 'Assimilation Era', when Aborigines faced ethnocidal restrictions and indignities imposed on them by governments. Hudson was fortunate however, in that he was still able to study his people's cultural traditions. Hudson is a noteworthy exponent of Aboriginal culture in that he has developed his talents across the full range of traditional and contemporary Aboriginal expressive arts. He has performed and taught music, dance, mime and painting, nationally and internationally, to children and adults. As well he is widely recognised as one of Australia's finest didjeridu performers and has recorded several solo albums as well as collaborating with various composers and musicians.

Hudson has gained a diploma in Recreation Studies in the tertiary education system and played a large part in the development of Aboriginal culture as an Australian tourist attraction. In 1987 he was instrumental in the formation of the Tjapukai Dance Theatre troupe, which has performed to many thousands of tourists at Kuranda, in northern Queensland and on overseas tours. The troupe has also won several tourism awards and is recognised as one of Australia's premier cultural attractions for overseas visitors. Hudson's talent on didjeridu features predominantly on the Tjapukai Dance Theatre's album *Proud to Be an Aborigine* (1989) which has sold in excess of 40,000 copies.

By virtue of his diverse artistic achievements and international profile, Hudson

David Hudson (1995).

has been one of the key figures in the Aboriginal cultural renaissance of the last decade. He has also been able to successfully export his expertise and enthusiasm and has been a frequent visitor to San Francisco, where the following interview was conducted. As the interview reveals, Hudson's multiple skills enable him to present a unique perspective on the didjeridu and its many and evolving roles as an instrument and icon. (*Fred Tietjen*)

FT: *Where are your people from?*

DH: My grandmother comes from the Guguyalangi people from a place near Laura, north west of Kuranda on the Cape York Peninsula of northern Queensland. I spent my early years on a cattle station. My mum worked as a cook. Those were some of my best times and had the most influence on my life. Some of my relatives were Aboriginal stockmen. They were around all the time and they taught me a lot of things. They showed me how to be at one with the land and they showed me dancing and culture in general.

FT: *Who has been the biggest inspiration and influence?*

DH: My mother was my biggest inspiration and the biggest influence on my whole life. She's such a strong-willed person. I'm so much like her. She watched me grow and she nurtured me and educated me in an important way. She's always said, 'You're an Aboriginal person. Be proud of who you are, you have something to offer the world.' And I believe that I have something to offer people around the world. And that's through music, song and dance. As long as I can remember, we always had a didjeridu in the house. When I started to play, I just played for my own enjoyment. I never knew that one day I would be performing didjeridu and presenting a cultural show for Australian people and audiences world-wide.

FT: *Have other people influenced you?*

DH: It wasn't until the early 1980s when I went to Perth, in Western Australia to attend college, that I met Richard Walley and Ernie Dingo and other Aboriginal people from the Middar Dance Troupe. Before I went to Perth, I think my circle was still broken and by going there, the circle was getting closer and closer. Those blokes helped me complete my circle. They inspired me about my own culture and encouraged me to explore my roots. From that experience I developed a greater awareness that as Aborigines we have 40,000 years of living culture to share. After that, I began to think about returning to Cairns Queensland and presenting a cultural show. That's how the Tjapukai Dance Theatre was formed. I had to share this experience with others and forming Tjapukai was the way to do it.

FT: *How did the didjeridu come to your people?*

DH: In my grandmother's country, when folks heard the sugarbag, little native bees, humming inside a log, they thought it was someone playing the didjeridu.

Richard Walley, didjerduist, playwright and Aboriginal 'Artist of the Year' (1993) – a significant influence on David Hudson's development as an artist.

But it was the sugarbag busily working making honey inside the tree. So the sugarbag led people to the didjeridu.

FT: *How would you describe the way you play?*

DH: Definitely strong and intense. I try to do a variety of things so I'm making the sounds colourful. I'm not just blowing a straight rhythm. Because in the background I'm always trying to accompany the strong rhythms with lots of guttural grunts and growls.

FT: *Who influenced your playing style?*

DH: Two blokes come to mind. I was influenced definitely by Dick Roughsey from the Lardil people. I am also influenced by David Blanasi from the Northern Territory.

FT: *What is it that distinguishes their playing?*

DH: Overtones, traditional grunts, traditional understanding of the bush and rhythms that are purely sounds handed down from one generation to the next generation. That's what inspires me, not just to pick up a didjeridu and just play any rhythm, but to play specific rhythms that mean something.

FT: *How do you compose a didjeridu song?*

DH: I get my inspiration from [nature]. For example, if I see a large bird flying in the air, be it a pelican, I imagine the pelican is using his wings, he's floating and his heartbeat isn't pumping very fast, he's just gliding through the air. He's soaring. [I] can imagine myself doing exactly the same rhythm as what he's doing. And the amount of beats that his heart's beating, [that's] exactly how I imagine my style of didjeridu playing to be. I play like the pelican is flying. I follow his rhythm.

FT: *Where do the rhythms come from?*

DH: Rhythms come from the land. They come from inspirations from water and inspirations from the wind. You go on a journey, you play the rhythm of being on walkabout and the rhythms of everyday life. You also play what you feel from your heart. That's a more diverse style of playing, instead of playing the one monotone rhythm you're adding other sounds to the didjeridu to make it more colourful. People who don't really understand the didjeridu sound may find monotone didjeridu very monotonous. If that's the case, you can start adding in animal calls and dingoes and kookaburra to make the sound more interesting.

FT: *What's the favourite song you've written?*

DH: I would have to say *Laura's Festival* on my album *Rainbow Serpent* (1994). That's just didjeridu. It just reminds me so much of the bush. And I imagine[d] a large gathering [at Laura] ... It's a time of meeting old relatives you haven't seen for a long time. It's a time of gathering and a time of sharing. That's why I mixed in some bird sounds and some animal sounds around me and that's exactly how Laura would [sound], so I incorporate the sound of the land in my playing of that song.

FT: *When you hear Euro-American people playing didjeridu, what do you hear?*

DH: They don't have that same rich, raw sound or that guttural sound happening. [They] play [in] more of a monotone rhythm, [they] don't use their voice box to get that really 'rrrghhh' [sound]. When you live in the country, you know how these things sound. You know how a dingo cries, in the bush, And how a kookaburra laughs. If you're a person from North America who's never heard a dingo before, how do you know what a dingo sounds like? You're trying to imitate something from a CD. To get the earth sounds and to get the richness of the bush sounds, you've got to go out and hear these things for yourself. There's no point in me trying to imitate a wolf, which I won't, because there are no wolves in Australia. You've gotta have that in you.

FT: *What have you observed about the didjeridu's use in North America?*

DH: I have seen people try to make the didjeridu into something different than what it is. They try to make the Aboriginal culture into something different than what it is as well. And if they don't know the facts, then they make it up. I've seen women players, instruments made out of PVC pipe and agave cactus and New Age 'Healers' [playing it over peoples bodies while making up stories about the didjeridu.]

FT: *Is the didjeridu used in any of these 'New Age' ways where you come from in Australia?*

DH: No. Not where I come from.

FT: *Do you have a sense of how and why these people invent these things?*

DH: Perhaps they're trying to find their own identity. I mean, it's amazing. They look to Australia, not to their own land. Why don't they relate to their own culture? Why don't they relate more to the indigenous North Americans? It's similar in Australia. It's amazing how Aboriginal didjeridu players get more recognition overseas than back in Australia. That's how I see it. People in Australia don't know how to relate to the indigenous culture in their own back yard. For example, if I asked the average Australian today to name five Aboriginal tribes, I can guarantee you, they can't name three. But if you ask the same person to name five North American Native Indian tribes, they can tell you quite easily.

FT: *Why do you think they do that?*

DH: Perhaps they place other cultures around the world as being more important than the original culture in their own backyard.

FT: *How do you feel about non-Aboriginal players of the didjeridu?*

DH: I think Aboriginal people have no problem with a lot of people playing didjeridu. It's only when non-Aboriginal people start being intrusive saying they want to be part of cultural things that are distinctly Aboriginal. I have heard people say things like, 'I want to part of the Goanna Dreaming or the Dreamtime'. Well, they're not Aborigines for starters. This sort of insensitivity just shows they don't know what they are talking about. If you've lived with an Aboriginal family and lived the way of an Aboriginal person perhaps then you'd have an understanding of the culture and be accepted in a deeper way. There's too many folks out there that get into this trendy mode and want to be Aboriginal. Aboriginal people have no problem accepting other people as long as they are themselves. Why try to be something that you aren't? Just be yourself. I'm a black person, I don't try to be a white person. I'm proud of who I am. I have my identity and I'm happy with that.

FT: *How do you feel about people in North America who are making didjeridus commercially?*

DH: Here in North America somebody makes an instrument out of PVC or agave cactus and they cost as much as $250. Why not buy the authentic thing? By buying the authentic instrument you support Aboriginal culture and help keep it alive. If an individual starting out can't locate an authentic instrument that's a different story. As a practice instrument, starting with a substitute instrument made of alternative materials could be the first step in a progression, with acquiring a real didjeridu as a final reward.

FT: *Do you think Aboriginal people should receive royalties when non-Aboriginal people copy their intellectual property?*

DH: Definitely. They owe respect and recognition to the indigenous people of Australia. If someone is making didjeridus in America from plastic pipes and agave cactus and they want to give recognition to Aboriginal people, probably the best way to do it is have the respect to come to Australia and meet Aboriginal people. Meet the elders and tell the folks what you're doing in America. Instead of just being in America and churning out PVC pipes.

FT: *What are the advantages of playing an authentic didjeridu?*

DH: The inside of a didjeridu has been eaten out naturally by termites. And all those little cracks and tracks that termites have lived in helps resonate that sound. It gives the didjeridu a warm, strong, earth sound. Something that PVC pipe can't create because these are all natural sounds, earth sounds. With a didjeridu you are playing a piece of timber that comes from an ancient land. It's been made and painted by an Aboriginal person. It has that feel about it. You can get PVC pipe from a hardware store. That's like playing mum's vacuum cleaner, you know? It's a black spirit that's within. The didjeridu has its own independent sound that's an ancient voice. It has charm that's quite mesmeric.

FT: *What do you mean by an 'ancient voice'?*

DH: Well, it's been made and played by Aboriginal people for thousands of years now. It's coming from the heart. It's coming from the land. It's a soul instrument. You feel it.

FT: *What advice would you give to Euro-Americans taking up the didjeridu?*

DH: This instrument has been played for countless generations. Play it from the heart. Play it for yourself. Give credit to the Aboriginal people of Australia. Don't take the instrument for granted or abuse it.

FT: *As a didjeridu player/dancer/songwriter/painter, what do you have to offer Euro-Australia?*

DH: 40,000 years of culture expressed through my art-forms. It's hard to compare 200 years of British and White Australian culture with 40,000 years of Aboriginal culture. [Just as] there is more to Australia than just meat-pies and kangaroos, blonde-haired people with blue eyes and surf-boards. There's more to the Aboriginal culture than the didjeridu. I want non-Aboriginal people to be proud of the original culture of Aboriginal Australia. Take away the didjeridu, you've got art, you've got women's business, you've got men's business, you've got ceremonies. You've got Aboriginal people living in the modern times. We drive cars and live in houses. There are a lot of folks that still think that when they see you [in traditional clothing and decoration] that's how you dress every day of your life.

FT: *How does the didjeridu connect to Aboriginal culture?*

DH: Just as Captain Cook's telescope led him to Australia, you can pick up the didjeridu and use it like a kaleidoscope and realise that inside the didjeridu, are the textures of a culture that is still alive. You have all these little tracks and paths from the termites and if you follow all the different paths, it will take you to the different aspects of the culture. You follow that path here and it will take you to the rock art. Follow that path here, that will take you to the ceremony. You follow this path here, it will take you to someone who is living in the 1990s.

FT: *What do you see yourself doing ten years from now?*

DH: I hope to see Aboriginal didjeridu recordings written down in musical notation. And taking that one step again. I would like to see the continuation of Aboriginal culture being re-lived and known throughout the world through cultural performance. That will be keeping it alive and taking the influence of Aboriginal culture to the next level again. It's a progression (socially and culturally). Aboriginal people were taken for granted and considered unequal, then we're accepted into the mainstream, then we're given the right to vote, then as we are becoming more powerful our voice is being heard around the world. So in this form, music will go another step again. And it will be another voice that will be there for many, many years to come.

Discography

David Hudson *From Campfire to Stagelight* , Enric, 1985.

David Hudson *Sounds of the Earth*, Fortuna, 1990.

David Hudson *Woolunda: 10 Solos for Didjeridu,* Celestial Harmonies, 1993.

David Hudson *Rainbow Serpent*, Celestial Harmonies, 1994.

Tjapukai Dance Theatre *Proud to be an Aborigine*, Larrikin, 1989.

Chapter Four

ACCOMPANYING THE DREAMING

Determinants of Didjeridu Style in Traditional and Popular Yolngu Song

STEVEN KNOPOFF

Introduction

Alongside impressions of kangaroos, koalas, boomerangs and a vast out-back, the image and sound of the didjeridu has fixed itself in the minds of people around the world as a symbol of Australia and of Aboriginal culture. This has become all the more so in the past two decades. People who have never seen or heard a didjeridu in traditional performance contexts may have encountered it in movie soundtracks or in recordings by small but increasing numbers of rock, jazz and new age artists who have taken up the instrument. As Peter Dunbar-Hall discusses elsewhere in this anthology, though often regarded as a pan-Aboriginal instrument, the didjeridu is probably indigenous only to certain areas of the north coast of the continent (Moyle, 1981). The didjeridu is called by different names in the various cultures that use the instrument. The didjeridus played by the Yolngu residing at Yirrkala, Northeast Arnhem Land, Northern Territory, are called *yidaki*.

Made from a variety of different woods, the didjeridu is simply a hollow tube. The instruments played at Yirrkala today are generally 1.3 to 1.5 meters long and made from the narrow trunks of stringy bark eucalyptus (*eucalyptus tetradonta*). The instrument maker does not hollow the tube, but rather seeks out a tree which has already been eaten out by termites. After the tree is felled and a proper length removed from the bottom portion of it, the bark and outer layer of wood are peeled and cut away. Some smoothing out of the inner surface of the blowing end and optional decorative painting completes the construction of an instrument.

In traditional performance contexts, Yolngu do not ascribe tonal pitch value to the sound of the didjeridu or to the interval forming between the didjeridu and the singer's voice. Accordingly, the precise tuning of didjeridus is unimportant in Yolngu culture.[1] The fact that Yolngu do not ascribe specific tonal pitch value to the didjeridu does not mean that the instrument's sound quality is musically unimportant. At each step in the process of making an instrument, attention is given to providing a sound that is clear and resonant. This is seen both in the discarding of tree trunks determined to be too dry to produce a resonant sound and in the use of a knife to cut away the outer layers of wood, which renders a lighter, more resonant sound.[2,3]

Different sets of playing techniques are found in cultures who use the didjeridu, but one universal technique is the production of a constant drone through the use of circular breathing. While blowing, the player retains small amounts of air in the cheeks; this air is then used to sustain the drone when taking quick breaths in through the nose. The basic blowing technique involves buzzing the lips in a way that is fairly analogous to Western brass instrument technique. One major difference is that the embouchure (the position and application of the lips on the mouthpiece of a wind instrument) of a didjeridu, while well-controlled, is less taut than the Western brass embouchure. The resulting greater flapping of the lips helps give the didjeridu its characteristic rich sound.[4] Additional techniques characteristic of Yolngu didjeridu performance include blowing the first over-tone; diaphragmatic accents (which tend to raise the pitch of the fundamental slightly); various types of tonguing; and vocal sounds, such as singing and guttural shrieks. These techniques are used in different combinations, simulta-neously affecting rhythm and timbre.

Musicological writings about traditional use of the didjeridu have focused on the cultures of Arnhemland and Grooyte Eylandt. In this literature (Elkin and Jones 1958; Jones 1967 and 1973; Moyle 1974; Stubington 1978 and 1984) discussions of didjeridu style have generally served two ends. First, basic playing techniques and characteristic rhythmic patterns have been described. Second, these descrip-tions of technique and rhythm have been used to contrast the style of one didjeridu-playing culture with another. For example, the eastern Arnhem Land style, which features rhythmic alternation between the blown fundamental and blown first overtone, is distinguished from the western Arnhem Land style, which uses only the blown fundamental pitch but achieves rhythmic variation through control of vocal resonance.

Discussions along these lines provide broad cross-cultural comparisons of style, but they do not explain stylistic variation within specific cultural areas. The stylistic use of the didjeridu by Yolngu players is particularly varied. Jones (1973) recognised this in stating that 'in the northeastern Arnhem Land area the various forms of blown overtone are added in, together with all the more western [Arnhem Land] techniques and the whole range of vocal effects already mentioned, producing an amalgam of possibilities that itself divides into many sub-styles'. (273) The range of techniques and rhythms employed by the Yolngu is not only varied, but applied in consistently patterned ways. In order to better understand these patterns of stylistic variation, a distinction is made between *style* and *determinants of style*. *Style* refers to the physical aspects of a player's sound and technique, including the use of particular techniques, rhythmic patterns, timbral quality and overall rhythmic 'feel'. *Determinants of style* refers to factors of performance that are external to the actual production of sound, but which may influence the manner of playing. Examples include the symbolic meaning of certain sounds or particular performance protocols.

The first part of this paper is concerned with the use of the didjeridu in the traditional Yolngu ceremonial song genre ('clan songs'). Clan song performance comprises a complex musical system in which didjeridu style is determined and organised by many factors. Didjeridu style in ceremonial clan song performance will be discussed in terms of seven determinants: physical determinants, performance protocols, ceremonial protocols, symbolic determinants, aesthetic determinants, developmental determinants and cross-cultural determinants. In the second part of the paper, some of the same determinants will be used to discuss didjeridu performance in the pop/rock songs of the Yolngu band Yothu Yindi. By contrasting the use of the didjeridu in these two different performance settings we may see both some of the changes brought about by the use of Yolngu didjeridu in a non-traditional context and some of the aspects of playing that carry over from the traditional to the commercial performance setting.

Yolngu clan songs

Yolngu clans *(bäpurru)* are groups of patrilineally related kin. Each clan owns an ancestral estate comprised of land, songs, designs, sacred words, ceremonies and ceremonial paraphernalia. The ancestral songs performed at public portions of ceremonies such as funerals and male circumcisions are referred to (in musicological literature) as 'clan songs' because each clan is associated with its own song repertoire. Each clan song repertoire embodies the ancestral history of a given clan and is marked by distinctive thematic, textual and musical elements.

During clan song performance, variably sized groups of men sing and accompany themselves with pairs of hardwood clapsticks *(biḻma)*, while both women and men dance. The performance also includes the accompaniment of one male didjeriduist (*yidakimi*), most often a young adult or teenager.[5] Ceremonial performances are built up from successions of hundreds of short verses (called *yutunggurr,* literally 'thigh'). Each verse typically lasts from fifteen seconds to a little over a minute and there are short periods of rest or conversation between each verse. The length of a given performance may vary from two or three hours to an entire day or evening, depending on the occasion.

Various ancestral spirit-beings associated with a given clan comprise the explicit subject matter of its songs. These spirit-beings include flora and fauna, natural phenomena such as clouds and wind, cultural artifacts (spears, canoe paddles, speech), great ancestral hunters and ordinary people. The words of each verse allude to some behaviour or quality of the spirit-being(s) in a particular ancestral context. The succession of song subjects over longer stretches of singing alludes to important events that occurred at particular places in the ancestral past.

Musically, clan song verses are commonly structured in three sections. In the first, introductory, section, the lead singer establishes the clapstick pattern, begins singing lines of text, or communicates (often in singing voice) information about the song to the other performers. The didjeriduist's entrance in this section often consists of a brief improvised passage that begins with one or two short staccato notes (a way of quickly adjusting the embouchure) and leads to a sustained note of variable length. While holding this sustained note the didjeriduist mentally prepares to begin playing an appropriate rhythmic accompaniment to the singer's melodic lines.

The second section comprises the main body of the verse. In its simplest form, this section involves a few lines of sung text accompanied by simple, unpatterned clapstick beating, an appropriate repetitive didjeridu pattern (vamp) and repetitive dance movements that represent some idiomatic behaviour or quality of the sung spirit-being. Frequently, the verse's main body is marked by a more complex inner structuring which might include the alternation between different clapstick and/or didjeridu patterns, the use of recurring vocal/instrumental refrains and/or multi-sectioned choreographic movement. At the end of the main body of the verse, the clapstick beating, didjeridu playing and dancing all come to a synchronised halt. In the third, concluding, section of the verse, singers may continue to sing lines of text, at this point usually in less metrically-bound phrases.

Clan song verses are constructed extemporally during performance, drawing from established sets of key song words, clapstick patterns, didjeridu patterns and dance movements. Clan song performance involves a significant degree of improvisation, particularly on the part of the song leader, who controls the flow from one song subject to the next, the choice of clapstick pattern and other aspects of performance. The didjeriduist plays an important accompanying role in the clan song ensemble. Together with the singer's voice and clapsticks, the didjeriduist establishes the rhythmic foundation of the verse. He is also frequently responsible for cueing structural changes within the verse for the benefit of the other performers. The song leader, however, is ultimately responsible for the shape and direction of the performance. The song leader is often a respected elder or middle-aged clan leader with a large knowledge of song texts and musical patterns and the ability to organise performances involving many people and a voice that can hold up during many hours of daily performance. The younger didjeriduist may be appreciated and respected for his musical skills, but his role within the ensemble is clearly that of an accompanist.[6]

Within the role of accompanist, the didjeriduist has a degree of freedom in creating appropriate patterns for sung verse. In many cases the didjeriduist's improvisation consists of slight variations upon a brief repeating rhythmic figure, or vamp. One basic vamp and two syncopative variants are shown in Example 1. In an appropriate performance context, any of these rhythms would be interchangeable; the use of one or another would not effect the perception of stylistic difference. Stylistic difference – differences in the 'way of playing' – is regarded here in two senses. In one sense it can involve particular aspects of rhythm, timbre and technique that are determined by various ceremonial or performance protocols. In another sense, stylistic difference may involve more general characteristics in a player's rhythms, rhythmic feel, or technique.

Example 1. Didjeridu vamp and variants.

Physical determinants of style

Both the physics of the instrument and human physiology are important stylistic determinants. Some of the physical characteristics of the instrument have been discussed above. The Yolngu's musical use of the didjeridu is impressively

Makuma Yunupingu of Yothu Yindi (1992).

creative, though by no means exhausts the sounding potential of the instrument. The western Arnhem Lander's rhythmic use of vocal resonance provides one example of didjeridu technique which is not emphasised by Yolngu players from northeast Arnhem Land. It is also possible to play the didjeridu in ways that are not part of any tradition today. For example, on most didjeridus it is possible, by tightening the lips, to blow two or more overtones above the two used by the Yolngu. Yolngu didjeridu players have developed and maintained a particular range of techniques that serves their functional and aesthetic musical needs.

Performance protocols as determinants of style

Some of the standard protocols of clan song performance directly influence certain aspects of didjeridu style. One of these involves the use of the blown overtone. In most clan song verses, the points where clapstick rhythmic changes take place and the point at which the instrumental parts come to a stop, are subject to performer discretion. In some circumstances the song leader or lead dancer provides these cues, but they are often given through the use of the blown overtone in the didjeriduist's part. In Transcriptions 1, 3 and 4 the overtone is used to cue the end of the instrumental and danced portion of the verse[7] (nb. all transcriptions are positioned at the end of the chapter). These types of cadential patterns are so ingrained in clan song performance that they are often used even where performance cues are not strictly required; for example, in cases where a set number of beats determines the end of a verse.

In cases where the didjeriduist provides performance cues, the song leader's preferences are still paramount. One of the didjeriduist's tasks as accompanist is to anticipate the number of vocal phrases the singer wishes to sing in a given verse. If the singer is unhappy with the point at which the didjeriduist cues the end of the verse, he may (during the break between verses) instruct the didjeriduist to sustain verses for a longer or shorter period of time.[8]

Another standard performance protocol that affects didjeridu playing is that different types of rhythmic patterns are appropriate to different clapstick patterns. The song leader changes the clapstick pattern every few verses within constraints related to the song subject. His choice of clapstick pattern, in turn, partly determines the range of rhythmic patterns a didjeriduist may use. Verses using slow, unpatterned stick beating – which Yolngu refer to as *bulnha bilma* ('slow clapsticks') – require a particular type of ametric didjeridu style. An instance of this is in Transcription 1, performed by Dhakaliny Yunupingu in 1990. One feature of rhythmic style with these slow stick patterns is that, in the absence of a regular meter, the singer's and didjeriduist's parts each cue forward motion in the other. Specifically, in the main body of the verse, the didjeriduist anticipates the onset of each new vocal phrase with two short notes (indicated by pairs of sixteenth notes in the transcription). The exact onset of new vocal phrases may, in turn, be influenced by the sounding of these two short didjeridu notes. (Note that the beginning of each vocal phrase in the verse's main body coincides with the didjeridu note immediately following the pair of sixteenth notes.)

This type of slow, unmetered clapstick rhythm is found in the repertoire of all Yolngu clans. Analysis of recordings since 1952 indicate that didjeridu accompaniments used to accompany this type of clapstick pattern are a well-conserved element of performance. Within this context there is room for only minor variation; for example, the use of one (versus two) brief notes in anticipation of a new vocal phrase. There are other classes of named stick patterns that are also accompanied by a restrictive range of didjeridu styles. These include *yindi bilma* ('big/important clapsticks', these are discussed in relation to ceremonial protocol, below); and, to a lesser extent, *ngarrunga bilma* ('walking clapsticks'), which include a variety of patterned and unpatterned rhythms in moderate (i.e. 'walking') tempo.

Ceremonial protocols as determinants of style

During lengthy public ceremonies there are times when song performance accompanies specific ritual events and less formal periods when the singing (and dancing) is itself the main event. Both ceremonial contexts have ramifications for didjeridu style. At important junctures during ceremonies, only a narrow range of song subjects, clapstick patterns and didjeridu styles is appropriate. For example, one periodic ceremonial event, called *gunbur'yun,* involves the calling out by one or more male performers of sacred names that connect Yolngu to totemic land sites. The songs that typically culminate in *gunbur'yun* are called *yindi manikay* ('big/important songs'). The clapstick pattern appropriate to both the act of *gunbur'yun* and the immediately preceding sung verses is called *yindi bilma* ('big/important clapsticks') and consists of rapid, unpatterned beating. The didjeridu pattern accompanying *yindi manikay* consists of a simple drone articulated by breaths (often pairs of breaths in quick succession) taken at fairly regular intervals, but without regard for the timing of the vocal or clapstick accents.

During less formal portions of ceremonies there are more opportunities for didjeriduists (as well as singers) to showcase more contemporary and/or personal styles. This may be seen especially in portions of informal performance devoted to 'newsong' verses (*yuṯa manikay*). Newsong verses comprise a unique sub-genre within clan song performance. Whereas all other clan song verses are believed to have been created by ancestral beings at the beginning of time and performed in the original manner to the present day, newsong verses are the acknowledged creations of Yolngu singers. Newsong verses are inspired by some contemporary event which, in the singer/composer's mind, is perceived in relation to an ancestral song subject. For example, on one occasion several years ago, a family got lost while driving home through the bush. This inspired the creation of a newsong verse concerning the ancestral dingo (who perennially wanders 'lost' through the bush). Innovative aspects of newsong verses may include invented text alluding to the contemporary event, new clapstick patterns and new rhythmic counterpoints worked out between singer and didjeriduist. New song verses are enjoyed by dancers and other ceremony attendees both because of their frequent rhythmic vitality and because of their longer duration (generally one minute or more, compared with fifteen to thirty seconds for most other verses).

Symbolic determinants of style

The sound of the didjeridu is usually heard as a simple rhythmic drone. At times, however, components of the sound – blown fundamental, blown overtone, or vocal effects – may take on specific symbolic meanings. For example, in particular contexts involving songs about Wuyal, the ancestral honey gatherer, the fundamental pitch of the didjeridu is understood to represent the drone of wild honey bees. In certain contexts, a long, blown overtone is sounded just prior to the start of each sung verse. Depending on the song subject involved, this sound could mean different things: for example, the cry of a dolphin or the call-to-performance of an ancestral didjeridu player associated with the Morning Star. An example of the latter may be seen in the long blown overtone at the beginning of the didjeridu part in Transcription 4. Short vocal shrieks produced simultaneously with the blown fundamental may be used at any time simply as means of creating rhythmic and timbral variety. When vocal shrieks are used in the accompaniment of text about any of a number of ancestral birds, the sound can be understood as symbolising the call of the given bird. Symbolic associations such as those described here affect not only listeners' perceptions, but also the players' selective use of particular techniques and sounds to accompany certain song subjects.

Aesthetic determinants of style

Some aspects of the didjeridu's sound reflect personal or group aesthetics. Personal and group aesthetics may determine both the general 'groove' or feel of the basic rhythmic vamp (including the relative placement of overtone accents on top of or behind the beat) and the relative complexity of specific rhythmic figures. Some didjeriduists gain reputations as stylistic innovators and over time may influence others' playing. In more than one respect, singers' aesthetics also influence didjeridu style. Song leaders frequently dictate certain didjeridu patterns or ways of playing that they want to hear. At the same time, a lead singer may be more, or less, tolerant of young didjeriduists' stylistic predilections. It is common for a didjeriduist to informally align himself, for a period of time, with specific singers. In this context, too, a singer may influence didjeridu style, because particular styles of playing will be worked out in the course of frequent improvisational and compositional collaboration. The degree of aesthetic openness or conservatism are traits that may also apply to entire clans. Some clans' newsong verse performances exhibit a wide range of clapstick patterns and didjeridu rhythms while other clans' newsong performances are more limited in their stylistic range.

Transcriptions 2 and 3 are excerpts from two performances of a newsong verse concerning an owl-like bird, tawny frogmouth. The two performances of *Tawny Frogmouth*, recorded thirty seven years apart, are by the same singer, Larrtjannga Ganambarr. This newsong verse was created in the mid-1930s by the singer's father. The two versions, though different in a number of respects, are identifiable as the same song by the use of a recurring three-bar refrain. The refrain is always sung on a single pitch (the tonic) and always contains the same text (texts are not indicated in these transcriptions). In both recordings the didjeriduist plays a different rhythmic pattern during the refrain than in the rest of the verse.

The earlier *Tawny Frogmouth* performance (Transcription 2) was recorded at Yirrkala in 1952 by Richard Waterman. The didjeriduist, Djirrnini Yunupingu, was a renowned player during the 1950s who featured prominently in Waterman's recordings. One aspect of Djirrnini's style is the alternate placement of overtone pitches at two eighth-note and three eighth-note intervals. The result is syncopated with respect to the regular two eighth-note figures of the singer. Another frequent, notable feature of Djirrnini's style (though not in the verse excerpted in Transcription 2) is a relaxed manner of playing and the use of light, distinctly behind-the-beat, blown overtones. These aspects of style may be heard in others' playing, too, from the 1950s through the present. The relaxed, behind-the-beat rhythmic feel is considered to be an older style of playing. It is rare in contemporary newsong performance which favours more precise, on-top-of-the-beat accompaniments.

The more recent *Tawny Frogmouth* performance (Transcription 3) was recorded in 1989. The didjeriduist, Gunybi Ganambarr, plays in a manner that is common in contemporary newsong accompaniments: the overtone is used for rhythmic syncopation, but the syncopation occurs within, rather than across, the beat; the rhythmic feel is not so relaxed as in the earlier recording; and the overtones are executed squarely in time.

Transcription 4 is of a complete newsong verse related to the 'Morning Star' song series, recorded in 1990. The didjeriduist, Dhakaliny Yunupingu, exhibits a style of playing that could be described as avant-garde. In the context of Yolngu didjeridu practice, the most striking aspect of Dhakaliny's style is the use of rapid staccato tonguing on the fundamental.[9] Additionally, Dhakaliny's style is marked at specific points by a complex rhythmic counterpoint to the vocal line and by a generally driving, on-top-of-the-beat rhythmic feel. Dhakaliny's personal aesthetic is readily discernible in the context of newsong verses, but not in verses associated with the stylistically constrained 'slow' clapstick pattern (see Transcription 1).

Development determinants of style

The way that Yolngu learn to play the didjeridu may help to influence both conservative and innovative aspects of accompaniment style. On the side of conservatism, Yolngu are, from childhood, continually exposed to the stylistic models of their elders. Once a young player begins to perform in ceremony, he is continually guided by singers and more experienced players towards the correct (i.e. extant) ways of accompanying various clapstick patterns and vocal phrasings. On the side of innovation, the impact of self-training and peer group interaction are both relevant. Though didjeriduists do not generally perform at ceremonies until about age fourteen or fifteen, experience with the instrument begins as child's play much earlier. Boys (and sometimes girls) as young as four or five may be seen ambling about blowing on small-scale instruments. Boys nearing performing age practice both traditional patterns they have memorised and new patterns of their own making. They accompany young would-be singers and, in informal technical duels with other young didjeriduists, they learn to push their skills and aesthetics to new limits. It may well be at this developmental stage that generational differences in style begin to take root.

Cross-cultural determinants of style

Since the establishment of a non-Aboriginal mining town (Nhulunbuy) near Yirrkala in the late 1960s, Western popular music (primarily in the form of commercial audio cassettes) has captivated Yolngu youth. Yolngu usually experience Western pop music as passive listeners, though, on occasion, a young didjeriduist may sit alongside a stereo cassette player improvising rock and roll rhythms in accompaniment to popular music recordings.[10] We can only speculate about the influence that this type of experience has upon ceremonial didjeridu style. However, on more than one occasion, a Yolngu commentator criticised performance involving contemporary and exuberant vocal and didjeridu rhythms by referring to it disparagingly as 'rock and roll'.[11] It is hard to imagine that there would be no influence. At least to this author's ears, the rhythmically driving feel of many contemporary newsong verse accompaniments sound more in line with a pop/rock aesthetic than earlier, more relaxed styles of playing. Whatever the bases of the shift in didjeridu style, the change itself is purely at the aesthetic level. The technology of the instrument has not changed; neither have the basic playing techniques nor the role of the instrument within the performance ensemble.

Yothu Yindi

Yothu Yindi is the most well known Aboriginal rock band in Australia today. Formed by Yolngu singer/songwriter Mandawuy Yunupingu in 1986, Yothu Yindi has achieved remarkable commercial and critical success for their culture-bridging, politically-conscious songs and performances. The band's members include Yolngu from Yirrkala and Galiwin'ku (another Yolngu settlement) as well as non-Aboriginal musicians. Their instrumentation combines standard pop/rock instruments (electric guitars, keyboards, drum kit) with Yolngu clap-sticks and didjeridu. Yothu Yindi's recorded and live performances include songs in Yolngu dialects and in English, with musical influence from three distinct genres: pop/rock[12], clan songs and a Yolngu recreational song form called *djatpangarri*.[13] Many of the band's songs are purely in one of these three styles, while some combine elements of more than one style.

The effect that performance context plays upon music style can be seen by considering the stylistic determinants in Yothu Yindi's didjeridu playing and in their selective use of the instrument. In the remainder of this section we will focus specifically on the stylistic use of the didjeridu in Yothu Yindi's pop/rock songs. These songs comprise the bulk of Yothu Yindi's recorded repertoire[14] and (compared with the band's recordings of clan songs and *djaṯangarri*) provide the greatest contrast with didjeridu style in Yolngu ceremonial performance.

In Yothu Yindi's pop/rock material the use of the didjeridu is made to conform to the performance protocol and aesthetics of the pop/rock genre in several ways: by the subdued presence of the fundamental tone in the overall mix; post-recording re-tuning of the didjeridu's pitch; avoidance of the blown overtone; heavy reliance upon the use of vocal shrieks for rhythmic fills; and the use of a strictly metronomic rhythmic feel. One of the protocols of pop/rock musical performance is the central role that the drums and bass guitar play in establishing the rhythmic feel of a song. The didjeridu and clapsticks would assume this role in clan song performance, but in the pop/rock context – particularly in sections where the bass guitar and lower-pitched drums are prominent – the didjeridu is relegated to a less central role within the ensemble.

Unlike the case with clan song verses where there is internal structural flexibility, all structural elements of Yothu Yindi's pop/rock songs are worked out prior to studio recording (perhaps with changes made in post-recording studio editing). In this context there is no need for the didjeridu to provide cues for other instruments. This is another reason for the didjeridu being less functionally important within the pop/rock performance context. Indeed some of Yothu Yindi's pop/rock songs do not use the didjeridu at all.

The lack of precise tuning of the didjeridu's pitches is a normal feature of traditional Yolngu song, but can cause problems in the pop/rock context. For non-Yolngu listeners, the presence of an arbitrarily pitched didjeridu together with electric guitars and bass could cause an unwanted perception of 'out of tunedness'. Because of this, in their pop/rock songs Yothu Yindi's studio engineers alter the pitch of the didjeridu's blown fundamental technologically in order to bring it in line with the non-Aboriginal instruments (usually to match the tonic or fifth note of the scale). A perceived need to re-tune the didjeridu in the pop/rock context is evident in remarks by Mark Moffit, recording engineer and producer on Yothu Yindi's album *Tribal Voice* (1991) 'when it's in tune it really makes a big difference with a rock track; when it's not it's a terrible sound' (cited in Neuenfeldt, 1993: 65).

The didjeridu's blown fundamental is treated in two ways in the pop/rock context. During portions of songs where the use of bass guitar is prominent the didjeridu is usually mixed down to the point of near or complete inaudibility. This allows the sound of the bass guitar line to come through unimpeded. By contrast, the rhythmic drone of the didjeridu is quite prominent in certain interludes where the bass guitar drops out. Thus, just as Yothu Yindi's entire repertoire is divided into traditional Yolngu and pop/rock songs, one finds that even within individual pop/rock songs music-stylistic distinctions can be made between sections that are more or less 'Yolngu-sounding'.

The didjeridu's blown overtone is scarcely heard in Yothu Yindi's pop/rock songs. As with the selective use of the blown fundamental, the even scarcer use of the blown overtone may relate to a desire to avoid conflict with the bass guitar. The blown overtone on Yolngu didjeridus tends to be an octave to a tenth above the fundamental (and so usually above the bass guitar range), but its sound would still conflict with the bass for two reasons. First, its tone, like that of the bass guitar, is deep and intense. Second, because the interval between the didjeridu's fundamental and overtone rarely corresponds to a Western tempered interval, it would be difficult to bring the didjeridu's fundamental and overtone pitches simultaneously in tune with the bass, keyboards and other guitars.

With the avoidance of the blown overtone and the restrictive use of the blown fundamental in Yothu Yindi's pop/rock material, the vocal shriek (superimposed on top of a scarcely audible blown fundamental or remixed together with a digitally sampled fundamental drone) is a major component in the band's didjeridu style. The sound of the vocal shriek is timbrally distinct but does not interfere with the primacy of the bass guitar/bass drum bottom. Two examples of Yothu Yindi's use of the vocal shriek may be seen in Transcriptions 5 and 6.[15] Transcription 5 is excerpted from the opening portion of the song *Dharpa* (Yothu Yindi 1991). Following a one bar introduction consisting of six vocal shrieks, the didjeriduist forms a rhythmic line that combines the fundamental tone with vocal shrieks. At the twelfth bar there is a general shift in instrumental texture. Here the didjeriduist uses only the vocal shriek (though a sampled sustained drone is audible in the background). This eight-bar section ends with a build-up of rhythmic intensity in the final bar. Transcription 6 is excerpted from an instrumental interlude in the song *Tribal Voice* (Yothu Yindi 1991). Here the didjeriduist uses only the vocal shriek. As in the previous example, there is a rhythmic build-up in the final bar of the interlude. One innovation in this section involves the use of multi-tracked didjeridu: one instrument sounds in the right channel, the other in the left.

The use of 'behind-the-beat' and 'on-top-of-the-beat' rhythm are both well established in traditional clan song performance, but only metronomically precise accompaniments are used in Yothu Yindi's pop/rock songs. In the popular music realm, metronomic rhythm is not only an aesthetic requirement, but a measure of a musician's competence. This view may be seen in Moffit's comments on Yothu Yindi's performance skills:

> ... *they are the heavyweight traditional musicians up there [Arnhem Land]; they're recognised as the leader and they play all the ceremonies. I've heard didjs before and it's quite easy for the player to get behind, to drag and this guy didn't* ... (cited in Neuenfeldt, 1993: 66).

Although Yothu Yindi does not perform at traditional Yolngu ceremonies, some of the musical decisions made by the band may be seen as following the same 'ancestral law' that guides traditional decision making. This includes making an effort to consult with and gain consensus among all interested parties before reaching important decisions.[16] In the case of Yothu Yindi this has involved consulting with clan elders regarding certain elements of their performances; for example, in order to gain permission to use ceremonial feathered headdresses in their stage shows.[17] At the same time, in order to 'cross over' into the commercial music arena, the band has consulted and worked with people who have experience and vested interests in commercial record production and distribution. Here, as we have seen, the perceptions and judgements of others working with the band (such as studio recording engineers and their perceptions of didjeridu pitch) have influenced Yothu Yindi's use of the instrument.

Didjeridu style in Yothu Yindi's pop/rock work is largely disconnected from the wide range of ancestral spirit-related symbolic associations found in ceremonial performance contexts (usually the calls of specific birds or animals). But in this same context there is a new, non-traditional association connected with the didjeridu's sound: for Yothu Yindi's non-Yolngu listeners, the didjeridu provides one of the main signifiers of the band's Yolngu identity.

Yothu Yindi's didjeriduists all learned to play the instrument in its traditional context long before Yothu Yindi was formed. These same musicians were also exposed to Western popular music from an early age. In this sense they, like all Yolngu, are bi-musical. The possible influence of Western popular music upon didjeridu playing in ceremonial clan song performance has already been discussed. In the traditional performance realm, such influences would be constrained by the need for the didjeridu's sound (and style) to support all of the traditional aspects of the performance genre (the need for structural cueing, the need to be aesthetically acceptable to elder singers, etc.).

In the popular music context, Yothu Yindi has been able to use the didjeridu in ways that would not be possible in traditional performance contexts. As we have seen, some of the band's contemporary didjeridu stylings involve the preference for certain traditional techniques (such as vocal shrieks) over others, the exclusive use of on-top-of-the-beat rhythmic feel and the alteration or extension of the didjeridu's sound through technological means. But the basic range of traditional Yolngu playing techniques has so far proven more than adequate for the purpose of performance with Yothu Yindi.

Conclusions

We have looked at several levels of clan song performance at which didjeridu style may be determined. These interrelated determinants are not an exhaustive set, but are simply intended to provide some filters through which the complexity of didjeridu style may be viewed. It is clear that Yolngu didjeridu style does not involve a single manner of playing. Rather, it is a variable aspect of performance, determined by aesthetic, functional and symbolic factors. In traditional clan song performance, didjeriduists (and other performers) enjoy a degree of creative freedom, yet the genre has, on the whole, proven to be a robustly conservative cultural practice. By restricting the contexts in which innovative performance may take place, Yolngu limit the effect of stylistic variation upon the musical system. The result of this circumscription is that the greatest degree of stylistic change affects the aesthetic realm of performance. By contrast, the functional and symbolic aspects of performance appear to remain constant.

In a number of ways, Yothu Yindi's adaptations to the pop/rock performance context can also be viewed with respect to traditional circumscription of musical style. In their pop/rock songs the possibility of multitrack recording and digital sampling and processing have allowed the didjeridu to be used in some very un-traditional ways. Similarly, aesthetic problems related to combining the didjeridu with Western pop instruments have influenced the more prominent use of vocal sounds. Neither of these factors, however, have altered the basic range of techniques found in traditional performance.

The circumscription of didjeridu style in Yothu Yindi's work can also be seen in the fact that their repertoire includes the use of traditional genres alongside (and sometimes within) pop/rock songs. In Yothu Yindi's recordings of clan songs and *djaṯpangarri* the use of the didjeridu is more or less the same as in traditional contexts. For young Yolngu listeners, there may be a double-sided message in this, namely, that pop/rock songs may provide an appropriate avenue for bridging cultures and experimenting with very new performance ideas; but traditional songs and performance – including didjeridu accompaniments – will remain strong and viable, even as Yolngu actively engage themselves in the creation of commercial music products.

Notes on music transcription

In Transcriptions 1–4, the vocal parts are given without texts on a six-line staff. The six-note scale upon which the vocal melodies are constructed does not correspond to Western scales because Yolngu tuning is both non-tempered and variable (i.e. the precise tuning of intervals need not be exactly the same from verse to verse or from performance to performance). Without concern for exact tuning measurements, the six lines of the staff represent each of the six discrete scale steps. The notes represented by the top and bottom lines of the staff are approximately an octave apart. The uneven spacing of the staff lines visually reflects the alternately large and small scale steps that comprise the scale. The sizes of these scale steps often roughly correspond to 3 and 1½ Western semi-tones, respectively. The vocal part in Transcriptions 1 and 4 use all six notes of the scale; the vocal parts in Transcriptions 2 and 3 use only the bottom three notes of the scale. For purposes of reference, approximate Western tunings of the vocal parts in these particular recordings are given on a standard five-line staff at the beginning of Transcriptions 1–4. Upward and downward arrows here indicate microtonal deviations of less than 1/4 tone from standard Western pitch.

All didjeridu parts are notated on two lines. The blown fundamental appears on the bottom line; the blown overtone on the top line. Circled noteheads indicate vocal shrieks sounding together with the blown fundamental. Dashed slurs in the didjeridu parts indicate the use of subtle, untongued articulation. In these cases, rhythms are created solely by changes in air pressure and shape of the oral cavity. For purposes of reference, approximate Western tunings of the didjeridu parts are given on a standard five-line staff at the beginning of Transcriptions 1–4. No didjeridu tunings are indicated in Transcriptions 5 and 6. In these excerpts the pitch of the blown fundamental is inaudible and no blown overtones were used.

In Transcription 1 only, vocal phrases are indicated by notes connected to a single beam. Beams do not indicate rhythm per se, but rather connect all the notes sung in one breath. Rhythmic notation of the didjeridu part in Transcription 1 is approximate and intended primarily as an indication of accented note grouping. Visual alignment of noteheads (vertically between the three parts and horizon-tally within parts) indicates relative attack points and durations of notes.

In Transcription 1, crescendo/decrescendo markings in the didjeridu part do not refer to dynamics, but rather to the relative amount of vocal resonance. The more vocal resonance that is used, the richer and buzzier is the resulting tone. In Transcriptions 1 and 4, double bar lines indicate the dividing points between introduction and main body and between main body and vocal coda. The *Tawny Frogmouth* newsong verse excerpted in Transcriptions 2 and 3 incorporates a verse/refrain structure. In Transcriptions 2 and 3, the double bar lines indicate the dividing points between verses and refrains. In Transcription 2, bracketed bars in the didjeridu part contain only approximate note values due to the lack of clarity in the original sound recording.

The transcriptions in this article were prepared with Coda Music Technology's Finale versions 3.2 and 3.5 for Windows.

Acknowledgement: The fieldwork for this study was generously supported by a Fulbright Award for Australia, research grants from the Australian Institute for Aboriginal and Torres Strait Islander Studies and an Andrew Mellon Predoctoral Fellowship. I would like to thank Gail Rein for commenting on an earlier draft of this paper.

Transcription 1. Dhakaliny Yunupingu, 1990
From Morning Star song series. Manydjarri Ga̱nambarr, lead vocal.
Recorded at Rorruwuy Homeland Centre, Northern Territory, by S. Knopoff.

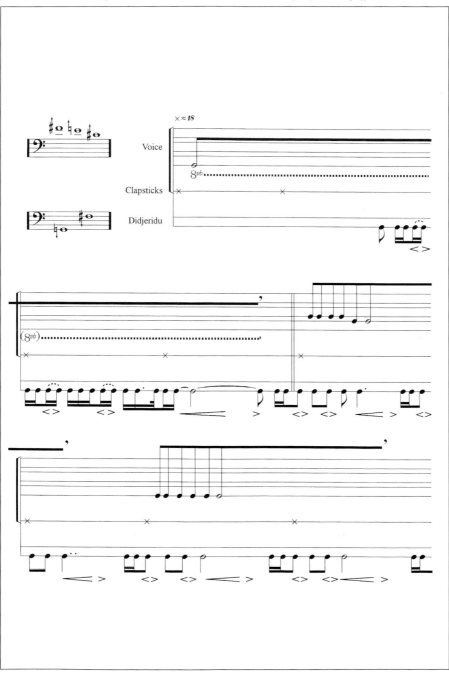

Transcription 1 (continued).

Transcription 2. Djirrnini Yunupiŋu, 1952.
From song about the tawny frogmouth. Larrtjanŋa and Waḏaymu Gaṉambarr, lead vocals.
Recorded at Yirrkala, Northern Territory, by R. Waterman.

Transcription 2 (continued).

Transcription 3.Gunybi Ganambarr (1989).
From a song about the tawny frogmouth. L̲arrtjannga Ga̲nambarr, lead vocal. Recorded at Yäŋunbi Homeland Centre, Northern Territory, by S. Knopoff.

Transcription 3 (continued).

Transcription 4. Dhakaliny Yunupingu (1990).
From Morning Star song series. Manydjarri Ganambarr, lead vocal. Recorded at Rorruwuy
Homeland Centre, Northern Territory, by S. Knopoff.

Transcription 4 (continued).

Transcription 5. Yothu Yindi (1991).
From Dharpa, Tribal Voice, *Mushroom Records.*

Transcription 6.Yothu Yindi (1991).
From Tribal Voice *(title track)*, Mushroom Records.

Notes

1. An analogous situation in Western music may be seen in the use of bongos or conga drums. These instruments produce quite audibly distinct pitches, yet we have trained ourselves to ignore the potential tonal relationship between these drums and other instruments in an ensemble. Instead we hear these pairs of drums as producing only relative 'high' and 'low' notes.

2. Didjeriduists in the Yirrkala area sometimes give pet names to instruments which acknowledge the sound quality of the instrument through association with an ancestral being. Magowan (1994), in discussing the naming of didjeridus in the Yolngu community at Galiwin'ku, notes that one didjeridu was named for the Olive Python, Wititj, because 'the twisted trunk of the tree was said to resemble the snake's body and the deep pitch could be likened to the deep and very powerful sound of the snake heard in the thunder ... [Another didjeridu] was named after a large swamp bird, the brolga, Gudurrku, as the player could produce a resonant brolga call from it' (283–284).

3. Tuning measurements of a dozen didjeridus recorded in the Yirrkala area in 1989–90 and 1952 show a range of fundamental pitches from 77 Hz (equivalent to a slightly lowered E flat one line below the bass clef) to 99 Hz (a slightly raised G on the bottom line of the bass clef). The intervals formed between fundamentals and first overtones ranged from 1226 cents (a slightly wide octave) to 1686 cents (a slightly flat perfect 12th), with the most common intervals falling in the range between a minor 9th and a neutral 10th.

    There is no indication that instrument makers test for specific musical intervals when looking for and constructing didjeridus. The approximate range of the fundamental pitch might be important, however, since very low-pitched instruments (which tend to be longer and have wider bores) require more air and are thus more difficult to play and because the overtone on very high pitched instruments may involve too much air resistance for the purpose of making graceful transitions between the overtone and fundamental pitches. There also seems to be some correlation between the relative height of fundamental pitches and the intervals between fundamental and overtone pitches. Specifically, the instruments with lower-pitched fundamentals tend towards slightly wider fundamental/overtone intervals while the instruments with lower-pitched fundamentals tend towards smaller fundamental/overtone intervals.

4. Wiggins (1985) discusses the role that 'loud, harsh' lip buzzing, vocal resonance and the naturally convoluted inner surface of the tube play with respect to the didjeridu's prominent high overtones and inharmonic formants.

5. At certain points during ceremonies, women perform clan songs as ritualised wailing, called *ngätji* ('crying'). *Ngätji* is performed by a group of women without clapsticks, dancing, or didjeridu accompaniment.

6. Some young men, through their clan lineage and/or song related skills, go on to become song leaders. For them, a period of time spent accompanying elder singers serves as an apprenticeship in singing and song leadership.

7. Unless otherwise noted, all transcriptions are from recordings made in the Yirrkala area in 1989–90 by the author.

8. The above discussion has focused on particular functional uses of the didjeridu's overtone. The reader should not infer from this that the didjeriduist's use of the overtone is completely determined by performance protocol, as this is certainly not the case. Throughout the main body of a song verse, alternation between the blown fundamental and overtone may be used to create rhythmic variety and in this sense the way that a player uses the overtone (as well as vocal shrieks) is very much a matter of personal style.

9. The assessment of these rapid staccato figures as strikingly unusual is based both on my own perceptions of Gakaliny's playing and on comments made to me by two other Yolngu didjeriduists.

10. Observed during my stay at Yirrkala in 1989–90.

11. Ibid.

12. The term 'pop/rock' is intended broadly to include all styles of English language songs – from country western and folk to heavy metal – that are disseminated via commercial recordings in Northern Australia.

13. *Djatpangarri* is a song form that developed at Yirrkala during the Mission era (late 1930s through early 1970s). In contrast to the religious, ceremonial nature of clan songs, *djatpangarri* songs are purely recreational in nature. Originally performed by young men at impromptu concerts at Yirrkala's beach camp, the subject matter of *djatpangarri* simultaneously concern a variety of everyday or contemporary phenomena (birds, the sea tide, cricket players, stage comics) while alluding to personal relations between individuals through reference to the names of particular secondary kinship groups (*mälk*) that the individuals belong to.

14. Sixteen of the twenty nine songs included on the Yothu Yindi albums *Tribal Voice* and *Freedom* are in a pop/rock musical style. The styles used in the remaining songs include clan song (6), *djatpangarri* (2), pop/rock and *djatpangarri* combined (3) and pop/rock and clan song combined (2).

15. The didjeriduists credited on the albums *Tribal Voice* (1991) and *Freedom* (1993) are Makuma Yunupingu, Bunimbirr Marika and Milkayngu Mununggurr.

16. Williams (1985 and 1986) has discussed the importance of consensus-building among interested parties in Yolngu decision-making.

17. Mandawuy Yunupingu, personal correspondence with the author, 1990.

Bibliography

Elkin A. and Jones T. (1958) *Arnhem Land Music* Sydney: Oceania Monographs n9.

Jones T. (1967) 'The Didjeridu: Some Comparisons of Its Typology and Musical Functions with Similar Instruments Throughout the World', *Studies in Music* v1.

Jones T. (1973) 'The Yiraki (Didjeridu) in North-Eastern Arnhem Land: Techniques and Styles' in Berndt R. and Phillips E. (eds)*The Australian Aboriginal Heritage: An Introduction through the Arts,* Sydney: Australian Society for Education through the Arts in Association with Ure Smith.

Knopoff S. (1992) 'Yuta Manikay: Juxtaposition of Ancestral and Contemporary Elements in the Performance of Yolngu Clan Songs', *Yearbook for Traditional Music* n24.

Magowan F. (1994) 'Melodies of Mourning', (unpublished D Phil thesis, Oxford University).

Moyle A. (1974) *North Australian Music: A Taxonomic Approach to the Study of Aboriginal Song Performances,* (unpublished) Ph.D. thesis, Melbourne: Monash University.

Moyle A. (1981) 'The Australian Didjeridu: A Late Musical Intrusion' *World Archaeology* v12 n3.

Neuenfeldt K. (1993) 'The Didjeridu and the Overdub: Technologising and Transposing Aural Images of Aboriginality' Perfect B*eat*, v1 n2.

Stubington J. (1978) *Yolngu Manikay: Modern Performances of Australian Aboriginal Clan Songs* Ph.D. thesis, Monash University.

Stubington J. (1984) 'Review of Djambidj: An Aboriginal Song Series From Northern Australia' *Australian Aboriginal Studies*, v1.

Waterman R. (1952) *Yirrkala Field Recordings* – mimeo (copies held at the Institute for Aboriginal and Torres Strait Islander Studies, Canberra).

Wiggins G. (1985) *The Physics of the Didjeridu* (unpublished manuscript, Boston University, College of Liberal Arts).

Williams N. M. (1985) 'On Aboriginal Decision-Making' in Barwick D. Beckett J and Reay, M (eds) *Metaphors of Interpretation:Essays in Honour of W. E. H. Stanner,* Canberra: Australian National University.

Williams N. M. (1986) *The Yolngu and Their Land: A System of Land Tenure and the Fight for its Recognition* Canberra: Australian Institute of Aboriginal Studies.

Discography

Yothu Yindi *Tribal Voice*, Mushroom Records 1991.

Yothu Yindi, *Freedom,* Mushroom Records 1994.

Chapter Five

CONTINUATION, DISSEMINATION AND INNOVATION

The Didjeridu and Contemporary Aboriginal Popular Music Groups

PETER DUNBAR-HALL

W hen the didjeridu was first used with the standard instruments of Western contemporary popular music by Aboriginal musicians remains unclear. However, the instrument's use in of popular music lineups has become a factor in assigning Aboriginal provenance and identity to a significant part of the recorded repertoire of contemporary Aboriginal popular music.[1] In this repertoire the didjeridu is used by Aboriginal performers throughout Australia. This is in contrast to the instrument's areas of use in Aboriginal traditional music, Arnhem Land and its neighbouring regions.

Interpretations of the presence and uses of the didjeridu in contemporary Aboriginal popular music offered here rely on identification of the instrument and the location of degrees and combinations of continuation and innovation. They also rely on a distinction between the instrument's traditional and later contemporary popular identities. Explanation of this location requires contextualisation of the didjeridu in time, place, musical type and socio-political perspectives. The context of time is crucial, providing two main frames: late 20th century Aboriginal culture and commercialised worldwide popular music trends. First, use of the didjeridu as an instrument of contemporary Aboriginal popular music on a national level occurs at the same time as a number of other factors of late 20th century Aboriginal history. Alongside the advent and political significance of pan-Aboriginality, the representation of all Aborigines as the one people, is a burgeoning of accessibility to and interest in Aboriginal cultures. Second, in the late 1980s, the didjeridu as a member of Aboriginal popular music groups is seen by some writers as belonging to the popular music trend labelled 'world music', a blend of 'mainstream and indigenous styles' (Sweeney, 1991: 8). Sweeney (ibid: 176–178) cites the use of the didjeridu by Aboriginal performing groups in this respect, listing under the world music rubric a number of groups who use it: Coloured Stone, Blekbala Mujik, No Fixed Address, Warumpi Band and Yothu Yindi. Knowledge of Aboriginal cultures, of which the didjeridu may be a musical symbol, can occur in this case through the disseminatory and commercial nature of the recording industry and agendas of popular culture.

The following discussion concerns the didjeridu as a member of contemporary Aboriginal popular music groups,[2] that is, groups which present themselves or are considered, as Aboriginal. Such presentation and consideration occur through a number of factors, including the naming of groups, advertising campaigns, song topics, the use of Aboriginal language/s in song lyrics and the intentions of performers as expressed in interviews and publications. This does not mean, however, that such performing groups are exclusively comprised of musicians of Aboriginal descent. Coloured Stone, Kulumindini Band, Tiddas, Warumpi Band, Wirrinyga Band and Yothu Yindi, to name only a few, include non-Aboriginal members. The uses and signifying potential of the didjeridu in this context are varied. Some understanding of them can be gained from examination of the instrument's musical roles. Through investigation of these roles it is possible to see similarities to and differences from the instrument's uses in Aboriginal traditional music, to link the didjeridu to movements in the broader Aboriginal community and to see the didjeridu as a site of continuation and innovation of musical and cultural practices.

Musical roles

According to Jones (1967, 1980b), as an instrument of Aboriginal traditional music the instrument commonly known as the didjeridu has a number of roles: as a drone, as a provider of tone colour, as a rhythm instrument, as a supplier of introductions, interludes and codas to songs, and as an issuer of elaborate coded signals. In a survey of recordings by contemporary Aboriginal popular musicians I identify six uses of the didjeridu: (1) as a referential effect; (2) as a drone; (3) as an antiphonal effect in conjunction with voices; (4) as a member of the rhythm section of rock groups; (5) as a soloist in the instrumental solo sections of rock songs; and (6) as the focus of rock instrumental pieces. None of these is mutually exclusive and a number of uses may appear within the one piece of music. In addition, developments concerning the number of didjeridus that can be played at the same time, and physical alterations to the instrument were noted. What follows is analysis and representative examples and transcriptions of these uses.[3]

For some performers, the didjeridu seems referential, appearing in a song when music in Aboriginal traditional style is quoted or when an Aboriginal topic occurs in the lyrics of a song. An example illustrates the first use. In *Treaty* by Yothu Yindi (1992) sections of singing in an Aboriginal language utilising a recognisably Aboriginal vocal timbre and employing a melody identifiable as that of the Yolngu[4] genre of the *djatpangarri*[5] are accompanied by *bilma* and *yidaki* (clapsticks and didjeridu, respectively, in Yolngu terminology). Presence of the didjeridu in these sections of this song can be interpreted as part of the process by which Aboriginal traditional music is referenced within a rock song.

A number of performers employ the didjeridu in a second referential manner, to illustrate or allude to Aboriginal topics in song lyrics. This can be observed in four songs by Coloured Stone. The instrument is not a regular part of this group's musical profile, appearing rarely on their seven albums and then often only in introductions (a signal of something Aboriginal?) and/or endings. When it does appear, its use is restricted to songs with specific Aboriginal reference, for example, in *Kapi Pulka* (1986), at the words 'listening to the sound of the didjeridu' the instrument is played. Similarly, in Roger Knox's (1983) recording of *Blackman's Stories*, a didjeridu imitating a dog barking is used when 'a dingo howling' occurs in the lyrics. For these performers the didjeridu illustrates mention of the instrument or occurs with Aboriginal topics or concepts related to Aboriginality.

The second use of the didjeridu, one that recalls a traditional use, is as a drone. This use of the instrument appears in music by numerous performers and performing groups. In what may be the earliest commercially recorded use of the didjeridu in a contemporary popular music setting, the instrument appears in the accompaniments to two songs, *Gurindji Blues* and *This Tribal Land* by (non-Aboriginal) Ted Egan, recorded by Galarwuy Yunupingu (nd).[6] In both songs the didjeridu provides a rhythmic drone, in *Gurindji Blues* alongside clapsticks: (Example 1 over) and in *This Tribal Land*, an acoustic guitar (Example 2 over).

In its differing combinations of voices and instruments, the recording of *Gurindji Blues* exemplifies the didjeridu as a site of continuation and innovation. The ensemble of voice, clapsticks and didjeridu heard suggests the same ensemble in Aboriginal traditional music described by Moyle (1981: 323):

> ... *the didjeridu is not normally played as a solo instrument. It contributes to a well integrated musical ensemble in which the chief participant, usually the song owner, sings as he beats together two hand sticks,*

Example 1: Gurindji Blues.

Example 2: This Tribal Land.

while the didjeridu in *This Tribal Land*, although playing a drone and thus recalling a traditional use of the instrument, works in conjunction with an acoustic guitar.

The use of didjeridu drones is a prevalent feature of music by the group Kooriwadjula (1992). The following example from *Truganinni's Lament (Old Black Line)*[7] shows this, in addition to unpitched notes and hooted upper partials as sectional markers at the ends of verses and lines of the chorus. Again, Jones' noting of the didjeridu as an issuer of musical signals could be borne in mind (Example 3: *Truganinni's Lament (Old Black Line)*, over).

In this example, the instrument has been fitted into the context of Western tonal music by its fundamental pitch being related to the tonal centre of the music, E flat. As in this song, appearance of the didjeridu in a contemporary popular music context often carries with it the alignment of didjeridu pitch to the functional nature of pitch in the Western tonal system. This is in distinction to the instrument's use in Aboriginal traditional music, in which the absolute pitch of the instrument may be unrelated to that of the vocal line.

This aspect of didjeridu use raises what is for some musicians a problem to be solved by mechanical alterations to the instrument. As it is generally understood, the didjeridu provides a fundamental note and possible upper partials, most notably a prominent one around a tenth above the fundamental. Among others, Mark Atkins (Kooriwadjula), David Hudson (Tjapukai Dance Theatre) and Adrian Ross have developed ways of altering the instrument so that the fundamental can be changed, providing the potential for the instrument to play in the key of any song and to change key within a song. These players have added moveable parts to the didjeridu, based on the principle by which a trombone works. Atkins calls his new didjeridu a 'didge-bone', Ross uses the term 'trom-doo' and Hudson, 'slide didgbone'. Hudson's is made by 'fitting together two PVC pipes, one inside the other' this 'creates a hybrid instrument able to modulate the pitch much like a trombone slide'. (Hudson, 1993, album notes).[8]

The third use of the didjeridu is as an antiphonal effect in conjunction with voices. In this use, the didjeridu plays at the ends of vocal lines where rests occur. This can be demonstrated by a quote from *Spirit of the Winter Tree* by Tiddas (1992) in which the didjeridu alternates between a drone while the voice is singing, and short rhythmic 'comments' (Example 4 over).

Short comments by a didjeridu in conjunction with a vocal line are relatively common throughout the repertoire examined, being a staple device in songs by Kev Carmody and by Yothu Yindi.

The fourth use of the didjeridu is as one of the instruments providing the rhythmic backing of a piece of music, in contemporary popular music normally a function of the electric bass, rhythm guitar, and drumkit. Again, a similarity to a traditional role ('as a rhythm instrument', Jones, 1980b: 461–462) can be noted. The

Example 3: Truganinni's Lament (Old Black Line)

Example 4: Spirit of the Winter Tree

assignation of this role to the didjeridu rests on a number of factors. In numerous pieces of contemporary popular music the didjeridu plays rhythmic and/or pitched one bar patterns or short riffs in conjunction with the electric bass. In other pieces the didjeridu plays rhythms usually assigned to the rhythm guitar. This can be demonstrated by the following passage from *Drangkinbala* (*Remix*) by Blekbala Mujik (1993). Here the didjeridu plays the rhythm known as a 'chicken scratch': single or pairs of notes on the second and fourth beats of a bar, often with a 'swing' feel (Example 5 over).

Consideration of the style of this song, the didjeridu's role in that style's identity and factors relating to Aboriginal traditional music exposes ways that the didjeridu's presence and uses in contemporary Aboriginal popular music can be interpreted on numerous levels.

The performance of the 'chicken scratch' rhythm is normally one of the roles of the rhythm guitar in reggae (see Davis and Simon, 1983); in which case for *Drangkinbala* (*Remix*), the didjeridu becomes a defining feature of the song's musical style. Reggae is generally considered an important influence in contemporary Aboriginal popular music. It can be heard in the music of many groups (see Ellis, Brunton and Barwick, 1988; Breen, 1989; Narogin, 1990; Castles, 1992; Dunbar-Hall, 1992). Use of reggae style in *Drankingbala* (*Remix*) reinforces an Aboriginal quality in the song which is already implied by the presence of the didjeridu as a recognisably Aboriginal instrument. In addition, the didjeridu's use as a rhythm instrument recalls one of its uses in traditional contexts (Jones, 1980b). Taken as a metonymic signifier, as a member of the lineup of this song the didjeridu exists simultaneously in three fields: Aboriginal music in general (by its presence), an Aboriginal traditional music role (by its rhythmic role), and a significant contemporary Aboriginal musical style, reggae (by its employment to play a specific rhythm).

Like the drumkit in popular music in general, and the didjeridu in some traditional contexts, in many cases the didjeridu in contemporary Aboriginal popular music plays short repetitive rhythms. Often these double, complement or are derived from those of the drumkit. In addition, the drumkit's role of sectional marker, provided through the playing of drum fills, is often taken up by the didjeridu. As with other roles of the didjeridu in traditional contexts which re-occur in popular music ones, the playing of sectional markers on the didjeridu in conjunction with instruments of the rock drumkit could be interpreted as a continuation of a traditional role. These characteristics of didjeridu use can be seen in Blekbala Mujik's *Nitmiluk* (1993).

Nitmiluk is constructed in three sections. The first is short and in traditional style. This is followed by a longer rock section, the piece concluding with the return of the opening traditional section. In the rock section of *Nitmiluk* the didjeridu

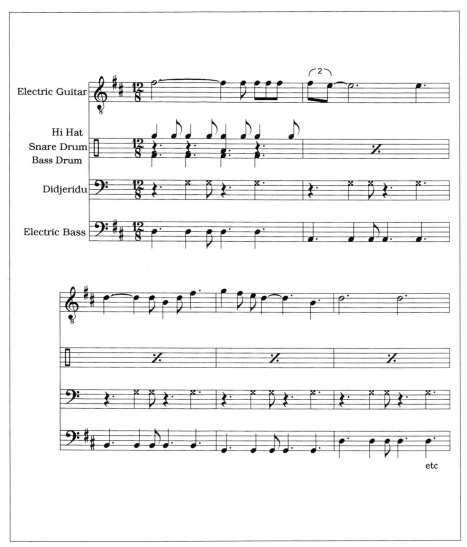

Example 5: Drangkinbala (Remix).

has four rhythms played in conjunction with a basic rock beat on the drumkit (Ex
ample 6: *Nitmiluk*: didjeridu and drumkit rhythms, over).

A fifth, two bar rhythm is used for a four bar instrumental fill linking sections
Example 7: *Nitmiluk*: instrumental fill, over).

In these transcriptions, the didjeridu can be seen as a member of the drumkit. Its
rhythms, like those of the drumkit, are (with the exception of that in the fill) of
one bar's length; these rhythms complement and integrate with those of the

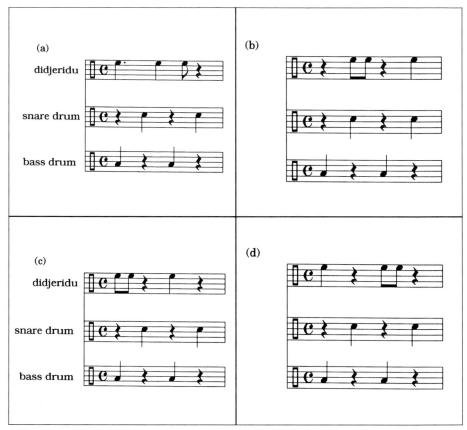

Example 6: Nitmiluk: *didjeridu and drumkit rhythms.*

drumkit; when the drumkit rhythms change to a repeated two bar pattern for sectional purposes in the instrumental fill, the didjeridu changes as well. Relationships between the didjeridu and instruments of the drumkit (the snare drum, floor tom tom and cymbal) in this fill are clear.

The fifth use of the didjeridu is what can be termed 'rock solo', in which the instrument replaces those normally assigned a solo section in the structure of rock songs, most often the (lead) guitar. In contemporary Aboriginal popular music this can involve performance by musicians recognised as virtuoso players, such as Mark Atkins (Kooriwadjula), Joe Geia, David Hudson (Tjapukai Dance Theatre), Bart Willoughby (No Fixed Address, Mixed Relations), Milkayngu Mununggurr and Makuma Yunupingu (Yothu Yindi).

Performance of didjeridu solo sections within contemporary songs is a practice of Bart Willoughby (No Fixed Address, Mixed Relations). A didjeridu solo by him in the song *Fight for Your Rights*, from the documentary film *No Fixed*

Example 7: Nitmiluk: *instrumental fill.*

Address on Tour (nd), is significant for a number of reasons. *Fight For Your Rights* is in reggae style. The insertion of a didjeridu solo into this song is one way in which that style has been appropriated by Aboriginal musicians. In this solo Willoughby speaks through the instrument: 'What do we want? Land Rights! When do we want them? Now!' As with the polysemous identity of the didjeridu in *Drangkinbala (Remix)*, the significance of this didjeridu solo can draw on connotations of style, the didjeridu's role as rock soloist and its employment as a channel for the delivery of a political message.

In the song *Tribal Voice* (Yothu Yindi, 1992), two didjeridus feature as soloists simultaneously. The following transcription from this song also makes the aligning of the didjeridu with the drumkit clear, for example, in bars 11 and 12 where the didjeridus play the same rhythms as the bass drum and then the snare drum for a two bar drum fill (Example 8: *Tribal Voice*: didjeridu section, over).

The sixth use of the didjeridu by Aboriginal groups is in a repertoire of rock instrumental pieces. As in the didjeridu section of *Tribal Voice*, the rock instrumental *Buffalo Stampede* (Blekbala Mujik, 1990a) uses two didjeridus, accompaniment being provided by the drumkit. One didjeridu (Didjeridu I) assumes the role of soloist using a combination of unpitched notes and an upper overtone, while the other (Didjeridu II) provides a low pitched drone accompaniment (Example 9).

Example 8: Tribal Voice*: didjeridu section*

Example 8: contd.

Example 8: contd

Example 8: contd.

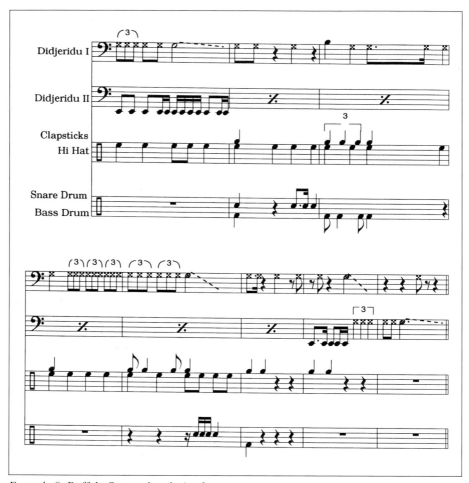

Example 9: Buffalo Stampede: *closing bars*

Continuation and innovation

A number of factors of didjeridu use in *Buffalo Stampede* demonstrate the concept of the didjeridu as a site of continuation and innovation. The first of these is in the use of two didjeridus at the same time, also to be seen in Yothu Yindi's *Tribal Voice* (Example 8). This contravenes what Moyle (1981: 323) had noticed in Aboriginal traditional music '(there is) never more than one didjeridu player'. (ibid)

Comparison of the playing styles of the two didjeridu parts in *Buffalo Stampede* shows continuation of a traditional playing style alongside an innovatory one. To understand this aspect of *Buffalo Stampede* it is necessary to consider the geographic provenance of its performers, Blekbala Mujik, and to compare the playing styles in *Buffalo Stampede* with those found in Aboriginal traditional music.

Researchers identify two didjeridu playing styles in Aboriginal traditional music. In west Arnhem Land the instrument is used to provide a rhythmic drone on its fundamental pitch, while in east Arnhem Land upper partials are used as well (Moyle, 1978; Stubington, 1979; Jones, 1980a; Knopoff, this volume). Blekbala Mujik are from Gulin Gulin, in west Arnhem Land. The use of a rhythmic drone for the lower didjeridu part in *Buffalo Stampede* recalls the instrument's traditional west Arnhem Land use, but the playing style of the upper didjeridu part, in which the upper partials are used, is an innovation for this area and for some listeners may be perceived as a reference to east Arnhem Land playing style.

While implications of playing style in this piece rely on identifying the performers' geographic origins and an understanding of traditional didjeridu use from that area, for performing groups outside areas of traditional didjeridu use adoption of the didjeridu is an innovation in itself, regardless of playing style or musical role. Introduction of the didjeridu into groups such as Coloured Stone, No Fixed Address and Mixed Relations, occurs at the same time as the taking up of shared symbols of a unified Aboriginal identity by elements of the broader Aboriginal community. The use of such symbols, the best example of which is the Aboriginal flag, is one part of 'a wave of feeling for "Aboriginal" identity' which 'seeks to establish a common socio-cultural heritage' (Berndt and Berndt, 1992: 528), despite Aboriginal linguistic and cultural diversity. Linked to this sentiment in late 20th century Aboriginal culture, use of the didjeridu by groups outside its traditional areas of use can be read as a musical form of pan-Aboriginality.

Interpretation of the didjeridu as a symbol of Aboriginality is reinforced by its appearance in the lyrics of *The Streets of Old Tamworth* by the late Melbourne Koori, Harry Williams.[9] Despite the song's explicit geographic positioning in an area far removed from those of traditional didjeridu use, the instrument is invoked alongside other images of supposed, shared Aboriginal culture in contrast to problems of the present and 'the whiteman's ways': the Dreamtime, corroborees, gumtrees, and the taste of porcupine.

> *The city lights are driving me crazy/*
> *As I walk the lonely streets of old Tamworth/*
> *How I wish that I was back there in the Dreamtime/*
> *In the country where there's always peace and quiet*
>
> *Oh I wish I was back in the Dreamtime/*
> *Hear the didjeridu droning in the night/*
> *Where the corroborees are seen in the firelight/*
> *Far away from the glow of city lights*

Now the old main street, it makes me feel so lonely/
For the gumtrees and the taste of porcupine/
I see my brothers and my sisters here in Tamworth/
Torn apart by government ways and city life

How I wish that I was back in the Dreamtime/
Hear the didjeridu droning in the night/
Where the corroborees are seen in the firelight/
Where the whiteman's ways won't bother me no more

(recorded by Roger Knox, 1993).

In a number of ways, musical uses of the didjeridu by contemporary Aboriginal popular music groups are not different from roles listed for the instrument in traditional contexts by Jones. The provision of drones, identification of the didjeridu as a rhythm instrument, its supplying of introductions, interludes and codas to songs and issuing of musical signals are all found in pieces of contemporary Aboriginal popular music. The musical context of contemporary popular music, however, includes new roles and uses of the instrument: membership of the rock group lineup, as a rock soloist, appearance in multiple numbers, developments in playing style, methods for altering fundamental pitch, and the aligning of the didjeridu with various instruments within the rock group. The last of these presents a means through which musical integration of the didjeridu into the rock group occurs. As a member of the drumkit the didjeridu performs as a rhythm instrument, often, as in traditional music, through the performance of short, repetitive rhythms. In addition it functions as an issuer of musical signals indicating sectional structuring of rock songs. In these capacities, conflation of traditional and contemporary popular roles of the didjeridu can be observed and the pivotal position of the didjeridu between the two musical types can be defined

Alongside these observations of the didjeridu's musical roles, the evolution of the instrument's significance as a generally accepted musical symbol of Aboriginal culture demonstrates ways that late 20th century agendas of Aboriginal expression have developed and been presented. Particularly relevant is the process through which an instrument of limited traditional areas of use has become perceived as an instrument typical of all Aborigines. The contribution of commercial record production and release and radio and television exposure are significant in this respect. Definition of the didjeridu as a pan-Aboriginal instrument is not, however, a foregone conclusion even on the part of Aborigines themselves. While Keeffe (1992: 51) describes the use of the instrument at camps organised to teach Aboriginal culture to Aboriginal youths in the 1980s as an appropriate activity 'of a traditional kind', acceptance of the didjeridu as such a symbol is not universal among Aborigines and use of the instrument can be a site of cultural dispute. Gummow (1994) provides an example of this in her description of attempts to include didjeridu lessons in a TAFE[10] Outreach Program for Aborigines in the Sydney south west area.

> *In 1988 ... I organised ... didjeridu lessons ... The teacher was from the Cape York area of northern Queensland and stated that women shouldn't play the didjeridu and that he would only teach the boys.*

> *After the second week of lessons, a senior member of the Land Council in Sydney stated that we should not be learning the didjeridu at all because it was not traditionally played in the Sydney area. He claimed that due to our didjeridu lessons he was now ill and if we didn't stop teaching, his illness would become worse. As a result we stopped immediately. However, the co-ordinator of the course was outraged. She stated that the didjeridu should be taught today in Sydney, an urban community with an urban background. According to her, the traditional rules don't apply in Sydney. Due to the disagreement the didjeridu teacher left and we discontinued lessons.*

Use and implications of use of the didjeridu as a member of Aboriginal popular music lineups are not uniform or one dimensional. Contexts of place and subsequent associations with Aboriginal traditional music, are particularly significant in understanding levels of continuation and innovation in the instrument's use and in indicating different ways in which the presence of the instrument can be understood. Alterations to the instrument to effect integration with Western tonal thinking and the evolution of new roles derived from rock music settings also assist in defining the dynamic nature of contemporary didjeridu playing. In these ways the presence of the didjeridu in contemporary Aboriginal popular music offers insights into cultural development, its presentation and manipulation.

Notes

1. See McKenry (1988), Breen (1989), and Stubington and Dunbar-Hall (1994) for comments on other factors in the assignment of Aboriginal derivation and identity in contemporary Aboriginal popular music. These factors include song topic, the presence of Aboriginal languages, popular musical style, and the integration of elements of Aboriginal traditional music with forms of contemporary Western popular music.

2. It is recognised that this is not the only context in which Aboriginal use of the didjeridu in forms of contemporary music takes place. Music in which an Aboriginal didjeridu player works with non-Aboriginal performers, for example a recording by Riley Lee (shakuhachi) and Matthew Doyle (didjeridu) (*Wild Honey Dreaming*, Lee and Doyle, 1993), a recording by didjeridu player Alan Dargin in collaboration with numerous musicians (*Bloodwood: the art of the didjeridu*, 1991), a recording of didjeridu player Johnny Didge and jazz group Batchelors of Prague (*Greville St Rock*, 1990), and a track on the Jimmy Barnes album *Flesh*

and Wood (1993) featuring Alan Dargin, are also examples of current uses of the didjeridu. They are not, however, central to this discussion.

3. Transcriptions show the number and type of voices in examples (f = female, m = male). Didjeridu parts are notated with a mixture of standard Western notation for pitched notes, and the following:

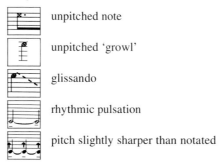

unpitched note

unpitched 'growl'

glissando

rhythmic pulsation

pitch slightly sharper than notated

4. Members of Yothu Yindi are Yolngu, from the northeast Arnhem Land coastal area.

5. For a discussion of this genre and its significance to the song *Treaty* and the Yothu Yindi album, *Tribal Voice*, see Stubington and Dunbar-Hall, 1994.

6. Galarwuy Yunupingu, a Gumatj clan leader, has been active in the Aboriginal Land Rights movement since the early 1960s. The date of this recording is not shown but is most probably in the late 1960s. *Gurindji Blues* is preceded by a spoken introduction by Vincent Lingiari, a spokesperson for the Gurindji in the1966 Wave Hill strike on a cattle station belonging to the Vestey family. The Gurindji demanded proper pay and conditions, and squatted on traditional land at Wattie Creek. The following year they unsuccessfully petitioned the Governor General for title to their land. The strike was one of the seminal events of contemporary Aboriginal politics, especially in relation to land ownership.

    The contribution of Simon Drake of the National Film and Sound Archive in locating this recording and bringing it to my attention is gratefully acknowledged.

7. Truganinni (d. 1876) was supposedly the last Tasmanian Aborigine. The use of her name is often a reference to attempts at wiping out the Tasmanian Aboriginal population.

8. Hudson acknowledges his introduction to this instrument by the non-Aboriginal didjeridu player Charlie McMahon. See Neuenfeldt (1993) for a discussion of tuning aspects of the didjeridu in record production.

9. 'Koori' is the term by which Melbourne Aborigines commonly refer to themselves.

10. Technical and Further Education: a system of public colleges for vocational training and community based courses.

Bibliography

Berndt R. & Berndt C. (1992, 5th ed) *The World of the First Australians: Aboriginal traditional life, past and present*, Canberra: Aboriginal Studies Press.

Breen M. (ed) (1989) *Our Place: Our Music*, Canberra: Aboriginal Studies Press.

Castles J. (1992) '*Tjungaringanyi*: Aboriginal rock' in Hayward P. (ed) *From Pop to Punk to Postmodernism*, Sydney: Allen and Unwin.

Davis S. & Simon P. (1983) *Reggae International*, London: Thames and Hudson.

Dunbar-Hall P. (1992) 'The Uses of Reggae by Aboriginal Musicians' (paper to Seventh Conference of the International Association for the Study of Popular Music, University of the Pacific, Stockton, California).

Ellis C., Brunton M. & Barwick L. (1988) 'From the Dreaming Rock to Reggae Rock' in McCredie A. (ed) *From Colonel Light into the Footlights*, Norwood (South Australia): Pagel Books.

Gummow M. (1994) 'Revival of Traditional Australian Aboriginal Music of New South Wales: performance and politics' (paper to Joint Conference of the Musicological Society of Australia and the New Zealand Musicological Society, University of Auckland).

Jones T. (1967) *The Didjeridu: Studies in Music*, n1.

Jones T. (1980a) 'Australia' in Sadie S. (ed) *New Grove Dictionary of Music and Musicians*, London: Macmillan, v1.

Jones T. (1980b) 'Didjeridu' in Sadie S. (ed) *New Grove Dictionary of Music and Musicians*, v3.

Keeffe K. (1992) *From the Centre to the City: Aboriginal education, culture and power*, Canberra: Aboriginal Studies Press.

McKenry K. (1988) 'Jacky Jacky: kicking over the traces' (paper to Third National Folklore Conference, Canberra).

Moyle A. (1978) *Aboriginal Sound Instruments*, Canberra: Australian Institute of Aboriginal Studies (companion booklet for recording, AIAS/14).

Moyle A. (1981) 'The Australian *didjeridu*: a late musical intrusion', *World Archaeology*, v12 n3.

Narogin M. (1990) *Writing from the Fringe: a study of modern Aboriginal literature*, Melbourne: Hyland House.

Neuenfeldt K. (1993) 'The Didjeridu and the Overdub', *Perfect Beat*, v1 n2 January.

Stubington J. (1979) 'North Australian Aboriginal Music' in Isaacs J. (ed) *Australian Aboriginal Music*, Sydney: Aboriginal Artists Agency.

Stubington J. & Dunbar-Hall P. (1994) 'Yothu Yindi's "Treaty": *ganma* in music', *Popular Music*, v13 n3.

Sweeney P. (1991) *Directory of World Music: a guide to performers and their music*, London: Virgin.

Discography

Jimmy Barnes *Flesh and Wood*, Mushroom, 1993.

Blekbala Mujik *Midnait Mujik*, CAAMA, 1990a.

Blekbala Mujik *Nitmiluk*, CAAMA, 1990b.

Blekbala Mujik *Come-n-Dance*, CAAMA, 1993.

Carmody, K. *Eulogy (for a black person)*, Festival, 1991.

Carmody, K. *Bloodlines*, Festival, 1993.

Coloured Stone *Black Rock from the Red Centre*, RCA, 1986.

Coloured Stone *Wild Desert Rose*, RCA, 1988.

Coloured Stone *Crazy Mind*, RCA, 1989.

Coloured Stone *Inma Juju*, BMG, 1991.

Alan Dargin & Michael Atherton *Bloodwood: the art of the didjeridu*, Natural Symphonies, 1991.

Johnny Didge *Greville St Rock*, Wishing Tree Studios, 1990.

David Hudson *Woolunda: ten solos for didjeridu*, Celestial Harmonies, 1993.

Roger Knox *Give It A Go*, Enrec, 1983.

Roger Knox *Warrior in Chains: the best of Roger Knox*, Enrec, 1993.

Kooriwadjula *Kooriwadjula*, Enrec, 1992.

Riley Lee & Mathew Doyle *Wild Honey Dreaming*, New World Productions, 1993.

Mixed Relations *Love*, Polydor, 1993.

Adrian Ross *Bridge the Gap*, Focus, 1994.

Tiddas *Inside My Kitchen*, Polygram, 1992.

Tjapukai Dance Theatre *Proud to be Aborigine*, Jara Hill Records, 1989.

Yothu Yindi *Tribal Voice*, Mushroom Records, 1992.

Yunupingu, G. *Gurindji Blues/This Tribal Land*, RCA, nd.

Film

No Fixed Address (nd) *No Fixed Address on Tour*, SBS TV.

Fig. 2. Eddy Watts [Barunga, N.T. Clan: Marla, Moiety: Dhuwa] Top design (banded section) represents body paint design, bottom represents sara-toga fish.

Fig. 1. Franki Li [Nunga from South Australia.] Design is South Australian Desert style and represents rainbow serpent in its many forms and colours.

Fig. 3. Bill Harney [Katherine, N.T. Clan: Wadaman, Moiety: Wulu] Top design represents arm and forehead bands for ceremony, bottom represents barramundi fish.

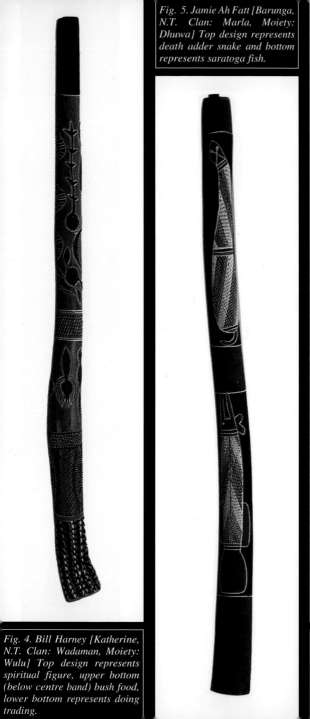

Fig. 5. Jamie Ah Fatt [Barunga, N.T. Clan: Marla, Moiety: Dhuwa] Top design represents death adder snake and bottom represents saratoga fish.

Fig. 4. Bill Harney [Katherine, N.T. Clan: Wadaman, Moiety: Wulu] Top design represents spiritual figure, upper bottom (below centre band) bush food, lower bottom represents doing trading.

Fig. 6. Farrely Dempsey [Coronation Hill, N.T. Clan: Remburranga, Moiety: Yirritjal Top design represents three dilly bags, centre boney bream fish, bottom represents barramundi fish.

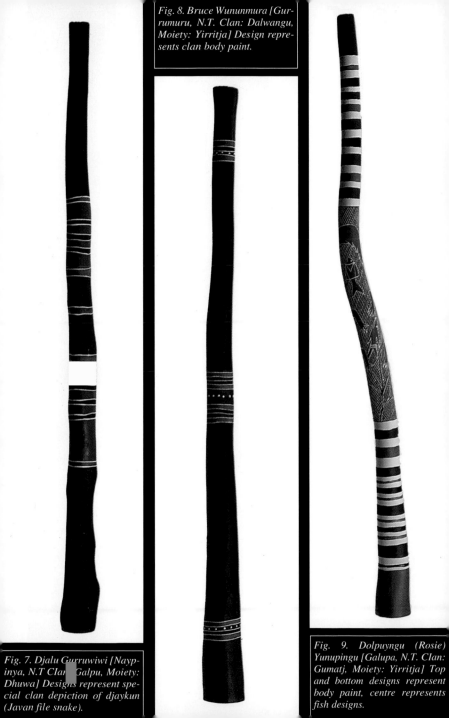

Fig. 8. Bruce Wununmura [Gurrumuru, N.T. Clan: Dalwangu, Moiety: Yirritja] Design represents clan body paint.

Fig. 7. Djalu Gurruwiwi [Naypinya, N.T Clan: Galpu, Moiety: Dhuwa] Designs represent special clan depiction of djaykun (Javan file snake).

Fig. 9. Dolpuyngu (Rosie) Yunupingu [Galupa, N.T. Clan: Gumatj, Moiety: Yirritja] Top and bottom designs represent body paint, centre represents fish designs.

Fig. 11. Opposite view of Fig. 9 by Dolpuyngu (Rosie) Yunupingu. Centre design represents crocodile.

Fig. 10. Artist Unknown [Gapuwiyak (Lake Evella), N.T.] Top design represents trading, next down special frog w_____res rain, next down loincloth for ceremony, bottom design represents rock cod fish.

Fig. 12. Tony _____ ilfred Warrgelark [Wal____ River, N.T.] Various cro_____ching represents particular landscape in artist's area.

Fig. 14. Artist Unknown [Gapuwiyak (Lake Evella), N.T.] Top design represents trading, next down obscured, next down special frog who makes rain, next down grinding stones for grinding food, next down special lizard who makes rain, bottom represents trading.

Fig. 13. Burrely Dempsey [Coronation Hill, N.T. Clan: Remburrang. Moiety: Yirritja] Top design represents ceremonial loincloth painted on top of bush food, bottom represents ceremonial head band painted on top of water goanna lizard's back.

Fig. 15. Djalu Gurruwiwi [Naypinya, N.T. Clan: Galpu, Moiety: Dhuwa] Top design represents clan body paint, bottom represents water lily.

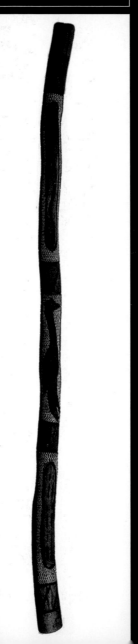

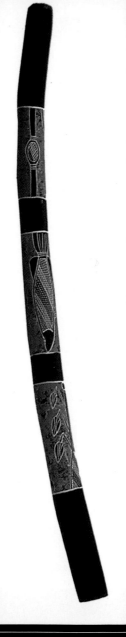

Fig. 17. Franki Li [Nunga from South Australia.] All designs represent the food chain. The animals depicted on the photographed side have their tracks depicted on the other side.

Fig. 16. Artist Unknown [Gapuwiyak (Lake Evella) N.T.] Top design represents barramundi fish, next down ceremonial loin cloth, next down campsite, bottom represents boney bream fish.

Fig. 18. Jamie Ah Fatt [Barunga, N.T.] Clan: Marla, Moiety: Dhuwa] Top design represents waterhole, centre the black bream fish, bottom represents the water lily.

Fig. 20. Eddy Watts [Barunga, N.T. Clan: Marla, Moiety: Dhuwa] Centre design represents a dancing brolga bird.

Fig. 19. Bill Harney [Katherine, N.T. Clan: Wadaman, Moiety: Wulu] Top horizontal design represents ceremonial arm bands, next down ceremonial forehead bands, next down loincloths with bush food, next down (half-circles) water lily roots, bottom represents 'knock-em-down-rain' (with hatching showing rain coming from different directions).

Fig. 21. Bill Harney [Katherine, N.T. Clan: Wadaman, Moiety: Wulu] Top design represents a boy's ceremonial arm band, next down a man's ceremonial arm band, next down bush medicine, next down body paint, bottom represents 'knock-em-down-rain'.

Notes: *There is a wide variety of decoration styles used by indigenous and non-indigenous didjeridu makers in Australia. The indigenous ones shown here represent only a few of them, but are good examples of decoration that is socially and culturally important as well as aesthetically pleasing. The details provided here are intended as general information only and are based on information supplied by the makers, where available. All reasonable efforts have been made to contact them. We regret any unintentional omissions or inaccuracies.*

Front cover: *The designs in Fig. 5 (Jamie Ah Fatt [Barunga, N.T. Clan: Marla, Moiety: Dhuwa]) also appear on the cover of this book..*

Acknowledgements: *There is a wide variety of decoration styles used by indigenous and non-indigenous didjeridu makers in Australia. The indigenous ones shown here represent only a few of them, but are good examples of decoration that is socially and culturally important as well as aesthetically pleasing. The details provided here are intended as general information only and are based on information supplied by the makers, where available. All reasonable efforts have been made to contact them. We regret any unintentional omissions or inaccuracies.*

Fig. 22. Bill Harney [Katherine, N.T. Clan: Wadaman, Moiety: Wulu] Top design represents a boy's ceremonial arm band, next down a man's ceremonial arm band, next down a Dreaming track connected to healing with bush medicines, next d (cross-hatching) arm bands, next d oincloths, next down (hor) forehead band, and bottom represents bush medicines.

Fig. 23. Norman Lane [Beswick, N.T. Clan & Moi y Unavailable] Vertical lines above the cross hatch at centre depict flower of water lily. When the flowers appear the water lily's tubers are ripe to eat.

Chapter Six

GENDER 'TABOOS' AND DIDJERIDUS

LINDA BARWICK

T his chapter aims to clarify some misunderstandings of the role of the didjeridu in traditional Aboriginal culture, in particular the popular conception that it is 'taboo' for women to play or even touch a didjeridu. While it is true that in the traditional didjeridu-accompanied genres of Northern Australia (e.g. *wangga* and *bunggurl*) women do not play in public ceremony, in these areas there appear to be few restrictions on women playing in an informal capacity. The area in which there are the strictest restrictions on women playing and touching didjeridu appears to be the south east of Australia, where in fact didjeridu has only recently been introduced. I believe that the international dissemination of the 'taboo' results from its compatability with the commercial agendas of New Age niche marketing.

My understanding of Aboriginal culture in Australia has been formed as an academic ethnomusicologist, through acquaintance with the ethnomusicological and anthropological literature as well as through personal contact, during classes and fieldwork, with Aboriginal people in a number of communities in South Australia, the Northern Territory and New South Wales. After presenting evidence that in traditional Aboriginal communities many women *do* play didjeridu, I will discuss some more general issues to do with the public modes of dissemination of information about didjeridus and my understanding of the role of the didjeridu as an icon of Aboriginal cultures in Australia.

It is true that traditionally women have not played didjeridu *in ceremony*. However, let us review the evidence for Aboriginal women playing didjeridu in informal situations. In discussions with women in the Belyuen community near Darwin in 1995, I was told that there was no prohibition on women playing and in fact several of the older women mentioned a woman in the Daly River area who used to play didjeridu. Greg Anderson has also reported that in a discussion with men from Groote Eylandt, Numbulwar and Gunbalanya it was agreed that there was no explicit prohibition in Dreaming Law that women should not play didjeridu, it was more that women did not know how to (personal communication, 1996). From Yirrkala, Steve Knopoff reports that while both boys and girls as young children play with toy instruments, 'within a few years, girls stop playing the instrument in public' (personal communication, 1996). Nevertheless, in July 1995 Knopoff observed women at Yirrkala playing didjeridu and singing for a performance of the non-totemic non-ceremonial *djatpangarri* songs (a secular genre usually performed by men) and he reports that women engaged in preparation of didjeridus for sale to tourists may also play instruments to test their useability (ibid).

Reports of women playing didjeridu are especially common in the Kimberleys and the Gulf regions, the westerly and easterly extremes of its distribution in traditional music. The didjeridu has only begun to be played in these areas this century (Moyle, 1974), where it accompanies genres originally deriving from Arnhem Land (*bunggurl*) or the Daly region (*wangga*, *lirrga* and *gunborrg*).

For the Gulf area, Alice Moyle's recording *Aboriginal Sound Instruments* (1978), contains a track, recorded at Borroloola in the eastern Northern Territory in 1966, of Jemima Wimalu, a Mara woman from Roper River, playing very accomplished didjeridu (track 1b, side 2 – see notes and transcription in Moyle, 1978: 17–18, 48). Elizabeth Mackinlay, an ethnomusicologist working with women from the neighbouring Yanyuwa group, reports women playing didjeridu, adopted recently from Mara people, in both informal and public performances (personal communication, 1996).

For the Kimberleys area, a woman didjeridu player is featured on the recording *Singing Up the Country* (1992) where on track 26, recorded in 1992, Polly Widalji plays a didjeridu solo (Garnduwa Amboorny Wirnan, 1992). In 1996, a Miriwoong woman resident near Kununurra in the east Kimberley, Annie Wilson, told me that she plays didjeridu for her own amusement, although she would not play for ceremonies or in public. Sandy Dann, a journalist and broadcaster resident in Broome in the west Kimberleys, occasionally plays didjeridu in schools and in private jam sessions and reports that elders in the Broome area have been happy for her to do so (cited in personal communication from Karl Neuenfeldt, 1996). Because of adverse reactions by Aboriginal men from other places, reactions that have become especially evident in the last few years, she feels that as an Aboriginal woman it is now inappropriate for her to play in public or for money and to teach the instrument (ibid).

Annie Wilson, Miriwoong people, Kununurra, Western Australia (1995). [Photo: courtesy of Fay Kijas.]

Gender differentiation in the use of didjeridu is consistent with the complementary division of roles along various gender and kinship lines that may be observed in many aspects of traditional life, including ceremonies, across Aboriginal Australia (Barwick, forthcoming 1996). In traditional ceremonies, women and men commonly use different parts of the performance space (both as spectators and as dancers), have distinct movement and dancing styles in performance and often use different forms of percussion accompaniment to singing. In general, in public mixed-sex ceremonies, women tend to use body percussion while men use instruments. For example, in Central and Northern Australia women commonly accompany songs by lap-slapping, while men use sticks or boomerang clapsticks.

Outside the area of its traditional distribution, didjeridus have sometimes been used by Aboriginal women for a variety of purposes. One of the more unusual instances is Maxine Fumagalli, a Noongar woman operating a business in

Denmark, in southwest Western Australia, who reportedly uses didjeridu for 'New Age' style healing. This involves the didjeridu being blown towards the body of the client and physical imbalances being diagnosed by changes in the timbre of the note (Sowelu, 1996). (This practice also takes place internationally, in contexts such as Amsterdam's Dreaming Healing Circle.)

Reports of the didjeridu being used by women to teach about traditional culture in Aboriginal education courses are more common. For example, the film *My Survival as an Aboriginal* (1978) shows Essie Coffey, of Brewarrina in New South Wales, using the didjeridu to teach Muruwarri children about Aboriginal culture.

It seems clear then, that reports of a traditional 'taboo' on women playing didjeridu have been greatly exaggerated. Nevertheless, the notion has become widespread amongst Aboriginal people in south eastern Australia and also amongst non-Aborigines both in Australia and overseas (see, for example, the Internet discussion in Thread One, following this chapter).

Much of the confusion surrounding the issue of women playing didjeridu is symptomatic of what Feld, after Schafer (1977: 90), has termed 'schizophonia', the splitting of sounds from sources through recording technology. This splitting has enabled the creation of the consumer product 'didjeridu music', which, along with many other types of 'world music', is marketed 'with few if any contextual linkages to the processes, practices and forms of participation that could give [it] meaning within local communities' (Feld, 1994: 259). In the case of the didjeridu, it is not only its recorded sounds, but the instrument itself, that has entered into the global marketplace.

With the recent international popularisation of the didjeridu through the global marketing of world music and the dissemination of instruments outside 'traditional' contexts, most notably through tourism (both national and international), the exchange of information about the instrument has taken place in a number of different media. Along with an interest in the acoustic qualities of the instrument and the techniques necessary to play it has gone an understandable curiosity about its cultural positioning in traditional Aboriginal culture. But such information may be difficult to come by and even more difficult to assess.

In many cases the casual tourist's main source of information on the didjeridu is from commercial sources – personnel in tourist shops, or recording liner notes. Here the primary concern is often with profit-making rather than with researching and accurately reflecting Aboriginal perspectives. For those who become didjeridu aficionados, information about the didjeridu is promulgated via public information sources such as the didjeridu list on the Internet[1] or other didjeridu web sites. Here, too, inaccurate information abounds.

Often the international marketing of didjeridu music, didjeridus and didjeridu lessons has been accompanied by a mystification and 'spiritualisation' of the instrument, in an attempt to tap into the lucrative New Age market. For example, according to the liner notes of *Wild Honey Dreaming* (1993), a recording of recently composed music for didjeridu and Japanese shakuhachi flute, the playing of both instruments is traditionally 'a most profound spiritual activity' (Lee and Doyle, 1993). In an informal survey I conducted in tourist shops in Darwin and Perth specialising in Aboriginal souvenirs in the period 1995–96, I found that the vast majority of didjeridu recordings for sale were of the New Age type, most recorded by non-Aboriginal performers and distributed by large multinational recording companies. Although numerous recordings of traditional Northern Australian music have been issued, few are available, their distribution is often poor and liner notes are often minimal or non-existent (see the annotated discography in Barwick and Marett, forthcoming 1996). Reputable recordings accompanied by informative notes do exist, such as the series edited by Alice Moyle *Songs of the Northern Territory* (first issued 1968, recently released on cassette and CD format), or Allan Marett's recordings of *wangga* singer Alan Maralung on the CD *Bunggridj-bunggridj: Wangga Songs by Alan Maralung* (1993), but are rarely stocked by souvenir shops. It is thus entirely understandable that many consumers of didjeridu-related products have formed quite erroneous impressions of the role of the didjeridu in traditional Aboriginal culture.

On the other hand, accurate scholarly sources of information are relatively difficult for the lay person to locate and read and often do not address the specific issues that have become prominent in recent years with the use of didjeridu in popular music and its international popularisation. For example, the entry on 'Didjeridu' in the *New Grove Dictionary of Music and Musicians* (Jones, 1980) deals only with 'traditional' Northern Australian didjeridu genres and playing techniques. It thus bears repeating here that didjeridu is traditionally played only in Northern Australia (and certainly *not* at Uluru, that other internationally-recognised icon of Aboriginal culture); that the instrument is associated with the public secular repertoire rather than with sacred ceremonies; and that archaeological evidence suggests that its use in Northern Australia dates back no more than one thousand years (Jones, 1980; Moyle, 1981). On the question of gender, the scholarly record is strangely quiet. While Jones' *New Grove* entry mentioned above states baldly that the instrument is 'played by Aboriginal men' (Jones, 1980: 565), he elsewhere acknowledges that 'some women' do play (Jones, n.d.). Alice Moyle's writings on didjeridu (e.g. Moyle, 1974) do not explicitly mention gender restrictions, but, as already mentioned, a female didjeridu player is included on her recording *Aboriginal Sound Instruments* (1978).

So, given the flaws and omissions of many commercial and scholarly sources of information, what of Aboriginal sources? It is important to understand that there is no single 'Aboriginal culture'. Throughout Aboriginal Australia there were once several hundreds of languages spoken, of which around one hundred are still actively spoken today (Horton, 1994: 1292–93). While most Aboriginal societies are governed by Dreaming Law, handed down through the generations in the form of ceremony and knowledge about people and country, that Law takes specific forms in specific places and there is no central authority. Indeed speaking without authority for other people or for their country or Law is problematic. For example, the Dumbartung Aboriginal Corporation's critique of Marlo Morgan's *Mutant Message Down Under* was issued only after extensive consultation with numerous Aboriginal communities in Central and Western Australia (Dumbartung, 1995). Traditionally, knowledge and the right to speak are negotiated face-to-face, in such a way that respect for the Law and culture is controlled and passed on as a personal duty of care rather than an abstract ethical obligation. Thus, sweeping generalisations about 'Aboriginal culture' are almost always fraught with difficulty. It is possible and even likely that different groups may hold quite different attitudes concerning issues to do with dissemination of information about traditional culture, especially in situations that are not clearly covered by traditional Law.

To some degree, all the world's citizens are affected (albeit differentially) by new technologies and modes of representation. For instances of the difficulties faced by Western cultures in assimilating and regulating the products of the burgeoning global market in music as cultural artefact, we might point to contemporary struggles in the international arena to articulate and enforce international copyright law in the age of sampling, or the problematic place of popular music studies in Western knowledge institutions. We should not be surprised then if there are a number of different responses in Aboriginal communities brought face-to-face with unprecedented outside demands for the products and the knowledge of traditional life.

For an outsider, it can be very difficult to reconcile these complexities. The situation is complicated further by the fact that the didjeridu has become an icon of Aboriginality, not only for outsiders, but also for many Aboriginal groups and communities attempting to construct a pan-Australian Aboriginal identity. Thus, in parts of Australia where didjeridu was not traditionally played (especially in southeastern Australia where the impact of European invasion and settlement has led to widespread loss of indigenous languages and cultural practices), Aboriginal people have recently begun to play didjeridu as a way of reclaiming an Aboriginal identity. In many cases it is impossible for them to reconstruct their own traditional ceremonial practice, so they have adopted and adapted music from those areas where traditional ceremonial life still flourishes, especially Northern Australia. For example, Matthew Doyle, an Aboriginal performer from New South Wales, learnt to play didjeridu through contacts with more traditional communities in Mornington Island (North Queensland), Yirrkala (northeastern Arnhem Land, Northern Territory) and Bathurst Island (Northern Territory) (Lee and Doyle, 1993).

Of course, Aboriginal people in southeastern Australia have a legitimate interest in international representations of Aboriginal culture and in many cases a particularly keenly-felt antipathy to the appropriation and commercial exploitation of Aboriginal culture by non-Aboriginal people. But other Aboriginal people hold contrasting views and see international dissemination of the didjeridu, and its use by non-Aboriginal women as well as men, as a way of raising international awareness of Aboriginal culture.

I mentioned earlier the use of the didjeridu for educational purposes by Essie Coffey, an Aboriginal woman from Brewarrina in New South Wales. In recent years Aboriginal women in New South Wales have come to feel profoundly ambivalent about such uses by women. In Coonabarabran for instance, an Aboriginal woman, Maureen Sulter, purchased a didjeridu to show to children in the school but carefully controlled its use. As she observed:

> *I got one and took it into the schools and I wouldn't let any girl, not even*
> *an Australian, a little kid, touch it. I said, no it's the law that no*
> *Aboriginal woman must touch it and I said I think the same thing applies*
> *to white society too. Today I won't allow any woman to touch it – or any*
> *little girl.* (cited in Somerville *et al.*, 1994: 26).

Many Aboriginal people in southern Australia hold to a view that a taboo exists against women playing the didjeridu, agree that it is inappropriate for both Aboriginal and non-Aboriginal women to play the instrument, and associate such uses with broader issues of loss and dispossession. For example, Walbira Gindin, Murri co-director for the Woodford Maleny Folk Festival held in Queensland in January 1996, cited non-Aboriginal women playing the didjeridu as an example of 'theft' of Aboriginal culture, accusing hippies at the festival of 'stealing the little that Aboriginal people had left to call their own' (Priest, 1996: 1). She is reported as saying: 'They have stolen our land, taken our children and now they want to take what little we have left – our songs, our dances and our art' (ibid). Perhaps a similar association lies behind Maxine Fumagalli's description of didjeridus harvested without due ritual as 'stolen babies' (cited in Sowelu, 1996: 17). In supporting Gindin's views, Bill Hauritz, Woodford Maleny festival co-ordinator, reported: 'One Aboriginal elder described it to me that whenever a non-Aboriginal person receives some Aboriginal culture it dilutes what is left because there is not as much' (Priest, 1996:1).

It seems that for Aboriginal people in southern Australia these attitudes derive from the widespread experience of loss of land, language and culture and the extraordinary efforts that people have made to protect what knowledge remains. In northern areas of Australia where didjeridu is traditionally played and where indigenous languages and culture are less under threat, there appears to be a more tolerant attitude to non-Aboriginal women learning didjeridu. For example, Jo Truman, an Australian composer and performer now resident in Europe, was taught to play and make didjeridus by George Jungawanga, a senior didjeridu player from Bamyili in the Northern Territory (personal communication, 1996). Similar reports of senior men teaching non-Aboriginal women in an informal way exist for eastern Arnhem Land:

> *A good friend of mine was first introduced to the 'didj' ... as an old car exhaust pipe while living at Nhulunbuy. She was riding in the back of a Toyota utility filled with people going back out to Yirrkala, when some of the old guys gave her a lesson in didj playing on the old rusted thing. She was amazed at their ability to make this old pipe come alive.*
> (e-mail posted on Internet list didjeridu@eartha.mills.edu, 6/12/96)

Such instances are not widespread. Most non-Aboriginal women didjeridu players are first taught the instrument not by senior men from traditional communities but rather through commercial channels, via tourist craft outlets or performance workshops.

Non-Aboriginal women players have reacted to the supposed traditional taboo on women players in a number of ways. Some interpret the taboo as applying only to Aboriginal women: as Kelli Young, a female didjeridu player and contributor to the Internet didjeridu list commented, 'I know it's taboo in the [Aborigines'] tribes but we don't count' (e-mail posted on Internet list didjeridu@eartha.mills.edu, 27/11/95). Other women upon learning of the 'taboo' have apparently given up playing, or given up playing in public (Jo Truman, personal communication, 1996). Still others adopt various other strategies to re-define what they do as outside the norms of traditional Aboriginal culture: for example, one North American woman plays the 'dreampipe' (a didjeridu constructed out of cactus), but was reportedly 'uncomfortable playing eucalyptus because of the traditional Aboriginal ban on women playing' (cited by Tom Keller, in e-mail posted on Internet list didjeridu@eartha.mills.edu, 19/10/95).

Similarly, Randy Raine-Reusch has stated that he chooses to play only plastic didjeridus in public because he believes that the didjeridu is a sacred instrument to be played only by initiated men[2] (e-mail posted on Internet list didjeridu@eartha.mills.edu, 28/9/95). The same writer expresses some of the bewilderment of overseas didjeridu fans who, having come to Australia to study didjeridu, are confronted with conflicting Aboriginal views:

> *Many players have told me that they studied in Australia and their teachers said it was ok to play the didj in public etc. I also studied in Australia and my teachers also told me the same, but I was also told by other people there that I really had no right to play this instrument, this was their instrument and it made them angry that I was playing their instrument. This was screamed to me in front of my teachers. But then everyone laughed and went on playing.* (ibid.)

If nothing else, the clamour of conflicting voices about the use of didjeridu by women and by outsiders has drawn attention to the potential for international exploitation and appropriation of traditional music and other Aboriginal cultural property. In addition, the debate has drawn to international attention the fact that there are levels of the sacred and the secret in traditional Aboriginal beliefs, many of them restricted according to gender. Perhaps the didjeridu in this case is functioning as a 'false front' (Ellis, 1985), standing in for other truly sacred and restricted aspects of Aboriginal ceremonial life that cannot be named in public. In this way, the 'spiritualising' of the didjeridu not only panders to the commercial New Age niche, but also serves as a means of warning non-Aboriginal people to be wary of inquiring too closely into sacred matters.

Acknowledgements: Thanks are due to many people for help in assembling the information for this paper. Karl Neuenfeldt generously shared his research materials. Jo Truman also gave invaluable help and feedback. Greg Anderson, Tamsin Donaldson, Jo Kijas, Steven Knopoff, Elizabeth Mackinlay, Allan Marett and Annie Wilson all contributed useful information. Finally thanks to Margaret Somerville and Allan Marett for reading and commenting on drafts of the paper.

Notes

1. See Threads One and Two, elsewhere in this volume, for examples of postings and interchanges on this list server.

2. For further discussion of Raine-Reusch's work see Neuenfeldt (1993).

Bibliography

Barwick L. (forthcoming, 1996) 'Gender: Australia', in Kaeppler A and Wainwright Love J. (eds), *Encyclopedia of World Music* (Oceania volume). New York: Garland Publishing.

Barwick L. and Marett A. (forthcoming, 1996) 'Selected Audiography of Traditional Music of Aboriginal Australia', *Yearbook for Traditional Music* v28.

Dumbartung Aboriginal Corporation (1995) *Bounuh Wongee 'Message Stick': A Report on Mutant Message Down Under* (co-ordinator: Robert Eggington), Waterford, Western Australia: Dumbartung Aboriginal Corporation.

Ellis C. (1985) *Aboriginal Music: Education for Living. Cross-cultural Experiences from South Australia,* St Lucia: University of Queensland Press.

Feld S. (1994) 'From Schizophonia to Schismogenesis: On the Discourses and Commodification Practices of "World Music" and "World Beat"', in Keil C. and Feld S. *Music Grooves: Essays and Dialogues,* Chicago: University of Chicago Press.

Garnduwa Amboorny Wirnan Aboriginal Corporation (1992) Liner notes to recording *Singing Up the Country: Traditional and Contemporary Songs from the Kimberleys, Western Australia.*

Horton D. (ed) (1994) *Encyclopaedia of Aboriginal Australia*, Canberra: Aboriginal Studies Press.

Jones T. (n.d.) Liner notes to the recording *The Art of the Didjeridu.*, Melbourne: Wattle Recordings, Wattle Ethnic Series n2.

Jones T. (1980) 'Didjeridu', in S. Sadie (ed), *New Grove Dictionary of Music and Musicians*, volume 2, London: Macmillan.

Lee R. and Doyle M. (1993) Liner notes to recording *Wild Honey Dreaming*, Red Hill, Queensland: New World Productions.

Moyle A. (1974) *North Australian Music*, unpublished PhD thesis, Monash University.

Moyle A. (1978) *Aboriginal Sound Instruments*, companion booklet for LP disc of the same title, Canberra: Australian Institute of Aboriginal Studies.

Moyle A. (1981) 'The Australian Didjeridu: A Late Musical Intrusion', *World Archaeology* v12 n3.

Neuenfeldt K. (1994) 'The Essentialistic, The Exotic, The Equivocal and The Absurd – The Cultural Production and Use of the Didjeridu in World Music', *Perfect Beat* v2 n1, July.

Priest M. (1996) 'Hippies steal our song and dance, say black artists', *Courier Mail* (Brisbane) 2/1.

Schafer M. (1977) *The Tuning of the World*, New York: Alfred A. Knopf.

Somerville M. with Dundas M. Mead M. Robinson J. and Sulter M. (1994) *The Sun Dancin': People and Place in Coonabarabran,* Canberra: Aboriginal Studies Press.

Sowelu D. (1996) 'Southwest Noongar Woman: Maxine Fumagalli', *Nova: Western Australia's Holistic Journal* v2 n11 (February).

Discography

Garnduwa Amboorny Wirnan Aboriginal Corporation, *Singing Up the Country: Traditional and Contemporary Songs from the Kimberleys, Western Australia*, Garnduwa Amboorny Wirnan Aboriginal Corporation and Production Function/Jovial Crew, 1992.

Jones T. (compiler), *The Art of the Didjeridu*, Wattle Recordings, Wattle Ethnic Series, n.d.

Riley Lee and Matthew Doyle,*Wild Honey Dreaming*, New World Productions, 1993.

Alan Maralung *Bunggridj-bunggridj: Wangga Songs by Alan Maralung. Northern Australia*, International Institute for Traditional Music/Smithsonian Folkways, 1993.

Moyle A. (compiler) *Songs of the Northern Territory* (5 record set), Australian Institute of Aboriginal Studies, 1968.

Moyle A. (compiler), *Aboriginal Sound Instruments*, Australian Institute of Aboriginal Studies, 1978.

Filmography

My Survival as an Aboriginal (d. Essei Coffey) (1978) Goodgabah Productions (available through the Australian Film Institute, Sydney).

THE ISSUE OF GENDER:

A Discussion on the Use of the Didjeridu by Women

KARL NEUENFELDT (ed)

The issue of gender in regard to the didjeridu is a complicated one. As Linda Barwick outlines in the preceding chapter, opinions vary within Aboriginal groups and within the many non-Aboriginal cultures where the didjeridu is now used. No hard and fast 'rules' apply. Although gendered preferences are present in some contemporary Western musical traditions, gendered uses of instruments are neither codified nor common. This is not so in many (non-Western) musical cultures however, where gendered uses are often connected to deeply-rooted secular and sacred rituals, celebrations and social or economic activities.

In February 1996 the following discussion appeared on the Dreamtime didjeridu web site and list service (didjeridu@eartha.mills.edu), lasted several weeks and provoked responses from Australia, Canada, the United States, Sweden and South Africa. It starts with a single, brief posting by a participant who then disappears, at least from the public discussion. The discussion reproduced below has been edited so as to highlight the principal viewpoints on women's use of the didjeridu (and a number of digressions are therefore excluded). As elsewhere in this volume, the original sequence, presentation and grammar of the thread is preserved to show the flavour of the on-line discourse.

I was wondering what all of you thought about women playing the didj.

Do you accept it or do you look down on it and even prevent women from touching the didj. as do some Australian Abori. (Stuart Gardner)

No problem. I'm not part of their culture so I don't feel any different about [it] *than women playing any other musical instrument.* (Dave Wallis)

My vote is based on my opinion; I enjoy playing my didj. I'm a man. I like to share good things with people. Women are people. I have read that Aborine hold special feelings about the didjeridu. All I know of that is what I read. All belief women should not play didjeridu. My feeling is different than that. My feeling and opinion and ignorance does not change Australian Aborigine belief. I do not believe my playing didjeridu is the same as the Aborigine's – like speaking words of a language I do not know. Play and enjoy. Evolution is still taking place. Other's feeling, opinions, beliefs and knowledge are to be respected. Who can say which minds will change? (Don Robinson)

... women playing the didgeridoo??? yuko! ewwww! next thing you know they'll cast a woman to play the part of the captain in a star trek show!!! no i'm just kidding ... . really i've not noticed that australian sexist thing about women and the didg here. in fact many women are on this list. it is a subject, though, that cycles up every so often here. speaking for myself there is no place for that traditional belief in the 20th century, in australia or america for anything!!! (John Pemble)

... My feeling is that the issue ... has been popularised by Western society, with little thought to the reasons behind it ... [In an Australian context] *I suspect* [that some Aborigines'] *vocal opposition to white women especially playing the didjeridu is motivated* [by] *their wish to reverse the power games that they have been subjected to for so long. And I suspect Western male didjers also enjoy a little power by advocating the use of didj by males only. So I would say to you, 'Go for it!'. Play it to your hearts content. None of us on the mailing list, I presume, are in any way tied into traditional aboriginal society, so all us are excluded from the context which governs aboriginal men's and women's social roles and obligations.* (Guan Lim)

All aboriginal groups have their laws and rules that everyone abides by. While these may appear to be sexest to some people, these are the norm for aboriginal people whether in North or South America or in Australia. In North America, our life style is not part of a tradition or custom that has been handed down through the generations as it has for many aboriginal groups. Therefore, to ask for an opinion on how one feels about women playing a gunbaark in relation to an aboriginal custom and tradition seems wrong in my opinion. (Lorenz Bruechert)

Hi, I'm a new subscriber, in fact this is the first thing I've ever subscribed to. Regarding the issue of girls playing the didg, I was under the impression that the didg was a male symbol. This then lead me to wonder whether there was any significance to the fact that a guy who plays the didg is called a 'puller', furthermore is it unreasonable to assume that when a female plays the didg one would call her [a] *'blower' Sorry I couldn't resist, I guess this isn't the best way to introduce myself ... I shall now go back to being a fly in the net ...* (Sean O'Regan)

... The first person I met with a real didj was a women and she gave me a few tips. This confirmed my male-dominant theory. Then I read up on the whole phallic aspect of the instrument and found out what traditional people thought. My opinion makes no gender difference, but if I run across some traditionalists, I'll hold my tongue. (Mischa David Krilov)

I have heard all kinds of stories about women and the didjeridu. One Aboriginal told me that women are not allowed to play because they will get pregnant. Another said it would make them infertile. Whilst I respect their beliefs, medically I cannot believe them ... Because of the variable stories ... I wonder whether the 'taboo' started as a rumour and has been perpetuated. Kind of like the Indian rope trick. The secret of the Indian rope trick is that nearly everyone has heard of it, but no one has seen it. (Guy Grant)

I was at a workshop in Melbourne ... among the wide variety of people present were several women ... so the inevitable was asked. The reply by David Blannasi [a Wugularr Northern Territory elder and didjeridu craftsman] *was basically that the taboo really applied to ceremonial use ... and interpreted appropriately would equally apply to any of us non-initiated-non-originals (or whatever it is that we should call ourselves). However, for the uses we derive, which Blannasi referred to as fun music, no such restrictions apply. This sounds to me to be an eminently reasonable way to deal with this issue.* (Martin O'Loughlin)

I can't recall when I've heard a more sensible answer [than Martin O'Loughlin's] *on a gender issue.* (Mischa Damon Krilov)

... well i think it's totally wrong for women to play the didgeridoo. just kidding. as one of two people in fayetteville arkansas who play the didg ... i would' love' to meet anyone else, male, female, alien, it doesn't

matter, who plays the didg. it's hard to learn from someone else when there is no one else. (Peter Horton)

... I think a lot of people have a notion that it is disrespectful to 'appropriate' the tools of the culture of a people who have been colonised and oppressed and then to use those tools in the style of the coloniser instead of in the style of the colonised people ... I think we need to distinguish between respect for another people's way of doing things and our need to develop our own appropriate way of doing things ... I also think it is possible to judge other cultures by the criteria you use to judge your own culture ... As to sexism in Didgeridu playing, I think it's entirely appropriate for us to make up our own rules. In any case, we will do that, whether its appropriate or not. (David A. Ford)

I agree with much of David A. Ford's opinion but I would also like to add to and disagree on some issues ... I think it is to our detriment to break tradition without understanding the tried and tested ... For indigenous peoples, I think that their adherence to their traditions and beliefs, with modifications as they see fit of course, as well as a good understanding of contemporary society is essential for continued prosperity. Because without tradition, identity is lost ... and without identity, many indigenous groups worldwide have had trouble coping with this new, strange world. Of course, living in and understanding two worlds is a difficult task and I for one have had trouble with regards this big ask (I am not of European extraction) ... Much of my approach to playing the didjeridu originated from somewhat humbling and slightly embarrassing experiences during my time in Ramingining, north-central Arnhem Land ... My good friend and ceremonial didj player (and I shall protect and honour his confidentiality) ... would take me aside [and] *instruct me, always patiently but sometimes annoyed at my slowness, in the finer points of didj playing ... At one point my friend* [related] *his experience of Darwin, of listening to a white busker* [i.e. street musician] *with a didjeridu and then follow*[ed] *with a mimicry of the busker to the hilarity of all present. The whole lot of us totally and absolutely cracked up at this rather derogatory playfulness. And then I began to think that what he demonstrated was indeed true and what's more, I was not much better than the average busker! So, although the joke was not on me, they were in effect, also laughing at me ...* (Guan Lim)

I don't know if my view is peculiarly American, or even peculiarly my own. I know that tradition plays a big role in identity, but I think that to suggest that without tradition, identity is lost, is to go too far. Here [on the use of the didjeridu], *I suspect, is where* [Guan Lim and I] *have our major disagreement. ... I don't think one has an obligation to understand how other's use the* [didjeridu]. *I do not assume that time-testing is the only valid test. I also believe that there is no appropriate role for outsiders to judge the music of another people ... I am using the didge in a manner that I think is appropriate for my cultural milieu. I would love to learn what it is like to play in the tradition of the didge, but that would be something else again. I am not trying to be an Aboriginal. I am trying to be, cliche though it is, me.* (David A. Ford)

David A. Ford, you and I have irreconcilable differences [with] *the role of tradition in present day and living culture ... I feel our differences in opinion arise from our vastly different cultural backgrounds. I assume, David, that you are of Anglo-Saxon descent and living a lifestyle heavily influenced by Western, industrial society. My* [Chinese Hokkien and Hakkah] *cultural tradition is quite different in many respects. Put simply, our cultural identity unifies us in all circumstance but especially in adversity. In contrast, my observations suggest that Western, Anglo society operates differently in a profound way. Here, personal identity is of supreme importance and individualism is the catch-cry ... My message is a simple one: the average Western didjeridu players can greatly increase his/her skill creativity, repertoire of techniques, etc. if s/he cares to take a little more than a passing interest in the 'old tradition' of playing the didjeridu ... And finally, I sincerely apologise for the story about the white didj busker. My feeling is that this may have caused hurt to most, if not all, subscribers and I am deeply sorry if this is indeed the case ... I merely wanted to illustrate that there is another dimension to didj playing and that there exists a substantial difference in style amongst the Yolngu.* (Guan Lim)

Guan, (if that is the correct way to use your name in the familiar sense) I'm one of the Anglo-Saxon, European stock, citizen of the USA and I don't find any need for an apology for the story you related. It was very funny to me. Let's face it, if we can't laugh at ourselves, when can we laugh? The dialogue is interesting too. (Carl Ramer)

An excellent expression of a very valid point and I commend you [Guan] *on taking the time to express and educate us all on a very important matter. Thank you very much.* (Adam Goldberg)

I'm quite new on the list and I am new with the didj to. I just want to say that I am surprised that there is womens on this list and playing the didj. I think it's good that there is intrested womens to! I can understand the abori. culture that say a women can't tuch it, if it say so. (I honestly don't know much about them, sorry!), that's there culture. But for us who don't have this culture it's un other thing. We chould not have such 'rules'. Have a nice time! (Gunnar Soderlund)

[Reply to Gunnar Soderlund] *I agree with what you are saying. We can respect that some aboriginal cultures have a taboo regarding women playing the didjeridu, but that doesn't mean it is appropriate for us (in our own, very different cultural context) to unquestioningly adopt that convention. There seems to be unanimous agreement on this issue from members of this list that have forwarded their comments so far ...* (Peter (I'llprobablygetflamedbigtimeanyway) Hadley

During 1988, 1989 and 1990 I taught the didjeridu through the Adult Education program in Tasmania. My classes were not gender-specific. Now someone is offering didj classes through Adult Education in Launceston ... But the ad in the paper expressly forbids women students. (Guy Grant)

I think that as we earnestly explore our interest in the didjeridu. It is a way to promote understanding and community. I feel that this list is a crucible in which to explore the diversity of our opinions. (Fred Tietjen)

Sometimes there is a fine line between describing one's point of view and saying something that makes it sound like you think you're better that someone else. But I don't think [Guan Lim] *you've crossed that line. Nevertheless, the issue of cultural appropriation* [of the didjeridu] *is an important one to me. I don't want to feel guilty for taking up the didj and I don't think I ought to feel guilty, even if I haven't been taught by an indigenous master. I believe that respect for all cultures is important, but I think it is possible to respect other cultures without making a study of them ... Sometimes it seems important to discuss the boundaries, to try to reduce the feeling on either side, that the other is trespassing.* (David A. Ford)

... I think the dialog has been interesting and a good example of how people can disagree with respect. (Peter Hadley)

At a surface level, there are several significant aspects to this Internet thread. One is that there appear to be no women or Aboriginal people taking part. Another is that the words 'Aborigine' (or 'Aboriginal') are most often used un-capitalised, indicating a lack of knowledge of contemporary Australian usage and cultural etiquette. At a deeper level, there are several further points of interest. One is a general lack of knowledge of/ interest in the significant historical, socio-cultural and political reasons why Aborigines would attempt to mediate use of the didjeridu, especially by the non-Australian participants. Another is that the thread overlooks entirely the question of who has the right to speak for Aboriginal people. Instead, in keeping with the general thrust of long-standing Western colonial perspectives on indigenous peoples, it privilege *signs* of Aboriginality above all else. The discussion relies somewhat unreflexively (but not necessarily disrespectfully) on a blend of mythology, travellers' tales and quasi-religious/spiritual conjecture. Somewhat surprisingly perhaps, the thread remains fairly civil even though participants express different opinions based on disparate world views, personalities and levels of information and knowledge.

Chapter Seven

THE DIDJERIDU IN THE DESERT

The Social Relations of an Ethnographic Object Entangled in Culture and Commerce

KARL NEUENFELDT

... objects are not what they were made to be but what they have become..
(Thomas, 1991; 4)

... in our age of commodity culture ... collective symbolic meaning is transferred to new generations not through stories, myths, or fairytales, but through things, namely the commodities we buy, sometimes sell and in a very limited way, can be said to produce. (Taussig, 1992: 55)

Introduction

Tourists alighting at Alice Springs hear the sound of the didjeridu. CAAMA (the Central Australia Aboriginal Media Association) employs a didjeriduist to entice passengers into its arts-and-crafts shop at the airport.[1] The shop sells commercialised Aboriginal artifacts such as bark and dot paintings, carvings, boomerangs and, of course, didjeridus.[2] The didjeridus and other Aboriginalia are bought and taken to far-off destinations as mementos of a particular time, place and situation, but also as ethnographic objects entangled in culture and commerce.

An idealised touristic experience of Alice Springs, the Outback and Aboriginal Australia often includes the sound and lore of the didjeridu.[3] However, its association with all of these is paradoxical. The chief irony is that the didjeridu is the major musical symbol of Aboriginality marketed in Central Australia, but it was not traditionally a hallmark of the rich musical traditions of local Aboriginal peoples.[4] It has only recently been produced in large quantities by both Australian Aboriginal and non-Aboriginal artisans, with a variety of constructions and decorations.[5] As well, most tourists are unaware that the surface simplicity of the didjeridu, even when adorned with exquisite paintings or used by gifted musicians, belies its depth of complexity. It has become a multi-faceted aural, visual and material icon of contemporary Aboriginality and Australia and the nexus of complex social relations.[6]

Theory and methodology

My inquiry is theoretically informed by two perspectives. One is Appadurai's (1986) analysis of 'things', that is, the social potential and social life of material objects.[7] The other is Thomas' (1991) analysis of ethnographic objects in the Pacific region and how use and assignment of value were negotiated and transformed by both colonisers and the colonised. These perspectives provide insights on mass tourism in locales such as Alice Springs and the attendant commoditisation and mass consumption of ethnographic 'things' such as didjeridus in a post-colonial context. My inquiry is methodologically informed by ethnographic interviews conducted in mid-1994 when I was one of the nearly half-million tourists who visit the Northern Territory each year.[8] To underscore the key role of social relationships, my ethnographic data privilege the often under-represented perspectives of cultural producers, within a more general field of cultural production.[9]

Overall, I provide a case study of the paradoxes and complexities that happen when the culture-in-commerce and the commerce-in-culture intersect in a geographical place (Alice Springs) and contest a textual space (notions of indigeneity) many equate with a particular 'race' (Aborigines). I contend that the advent and efflorescence of the didjeridu in the desert is neither accidental nor unusual. It is a predictable point of convergence for some of the major aesthetic, economic, socio-cultural and political trends of the late 20th century: a point of convergence wherein a musical instrument of limited historical distribution has been globalised to become, for some users and audiences, a metonym for Aboriginal culture or indigeneity as an abstract whole.[10]

The ethnographic data

To understand some of the paradoxes and complexities surrounding the didjeridu in the desert, I present my ethnographic data to show how the didjeridu is talked about as well as how the social relationships of cultural production are conceptualised by participants. The brief excerpts focus on the economic, technological, aesthetic, media, interpersonal and ideological facets of cultural production of those who create and co-habitate an art world, in which the efforts of many people contribute to an art-work. Even though participants in the didjeridu art world may operate anonymously and in relative isolation from each other and within asymmetrical power-knowledge relations, the thing they produce is a joint effort.[11]

The informants cited in this chapter were interviewed in 1994 and were living at that time in Alice Springs, although most are originally from elsewhere. They are included here because they are broadly representative of the types of social actors, agendas and alliances involved in the didjeridu's cultural production. The Aboriginal informants are Owen Cole, the general manager of CAAMA; Art Nickolls, a performer and retailer; and Stan Satour, an engineer and producer with CAAMA. The non-Aboriginal informants are Andrew Langford, performer and co-owner of the Original Dreamtime Gallery; Richard Micaleff, manager of the CAAMA record label; and Ross Muir, a recording engineer. (All interview extracts are indicated by the abbreviation 'i/v').

The economic facet

The economic facet of cultural production is tied into macro-economic flows of the global cultural economy, such as the movement of currencies associated with mass-tourism and of capital associated with transnational tourism development. However, I focus here on a more micro-economic level; the experiences of the social actors involved in retailing and performance within the local economy. To give some idea of the scope of the local didjeridu industry, the mail-room manager of Australia Post in Alice Springs has stated that 'a big mob of didjs go out ... sometimes van loads'[12] and estimates between 50–100 have been shipped per week over the last seven years. They are wrapped in paper or bubble-pack and make up 50 per cent of the Aboriginalia mailed out of Alice Springs.

Art Nickolls is in the unique position of being involved in both retailing and performance. Nickolls is the didjeridu player, referred to at the beginning of this chapter, who performs in the Alice Springs airport for tourists. In a good week the shop sells 10 didjeridus ranging in price from $180–380 (Australian):

> *I do it for the CAAMA* [Aboriginal Arts and Crafts] *shop ... right in the middle of the airport. As soon as people walk off the planes, I play and*

*Andrew Langford and didjeridus in The Original Dreamtime
Gallery. [Photographer: Rosemary Penrose.]*

attract them into the shop and hopefully sell a didj and some other
[Aboriginal] *things.* (i/v)

The performance situation is atypical:

*If the people stand around and they want to have a listen for a while,
then I'll probably play for about 5 minutes, 10 minutes all up ... If
particular people are interested, I go through and talk more to them, go
through different didjeridus and explain why certain things are* [differ-
ent]. *For example, we have a mixture of some that have got the 'top-end'
traditional decoration style ... and then also the new sort of stuff with dot
paintings. CAAMA has got Aboriginal artists so they just get the didjeridus sent over unfinished and then paint them themselves. I think that's
pretty unique to Alice Springs.* (i/v)

Andrew Langford is intimately involved in the local economy of the didjeridu as
a performer, recording artist and co-proprietor of The Original Dreamtime

Gallery. He acknowledges that as a retailer he sometimes acts as a de facto culture broker, especially when making aesthetic judgements in choosing which didjeridus to sell. This is a consideration because his store tends towards more traditional styles and colours in the crafts, paintings and didjeridus he sells to tourists, museums and galleries interstate and overseas:

> *I suppose I have to act as a cultural broker at times. There's a lot of different, contemporary styles come out, whether it's paintings or didjeridus. Being a proprietor ... some things I might find easier to sell because they fit in. With some artists we couldn't sell their work. It wouldn't fit in with our 'look'.* (i/v)

Langford notes that Alice Springs has decided advantages for retailing: 'we are just in a better tourist location than Darwin or other places where they probably sell didjeridus but just don't get the same sort of track-flow of people moving through' (i/v).

Richard Micaleff surmises that there exists a large, relatively untapped market for didjeridu music per se in Australian tourist outlets, as well as more generally in the marketing genre of world music. As a manufacturer and marketer of Aboriginal music, CAAMA's record label has to meet the conventional demands of the recording industry as well as several distinctive ones, such as what happens when an Aboriginal recording artist passes away and the use of culturally appropriate contracts.

> *If we have the death of someone ... then basically we have to withdraw any product until the family gives permission. The process will involve a period of mourning and a period of reconciliation within the family. They would be offended if they heard the music or heard the name mentioned, so we refer to people, even other people with the same first name, as Kumanjayi, a generic term for 'a person who has passed away' ... Occasionally we do a foray, perhaps through a member of CAAMA's governing committee and sensitively sound out whether it's the appropriate moment ... But if it's too difficult, the marketing period for that product may have passed, so we'll just let it go.* (i/v)

As to contracts, Micaleff says that the CAAMA record label adheres to standard music industry contracts, but also is sensitive to other issues:

> *One of the ways of marketing is to create appropriate products and our contracts are appropriate to cultural copyright issues and to the specific needs of Aboriginal artists. For example, with some traditional music ... we are still able to work with and market a recording whilst the artist or community retains the copyright.* (i/v)

111

Micaleff also feels the CAAMA record label has a particular role in the local and national, economy as 'part of the infrastructure of the emerging of Aboriginal culture', although being isolated in the middle of the continent can be a challenge:

> *Like any other record label, if you're not out there pushing, you get forgotten. And you're in Alice Springs, so who cares! But Aboriginal people care and I think it's something perhaps almost symbolic* [because] *Alice Springs* [is] *the heartland* [of the central desert region] *... and many urban Aborigines have families originating from here and from other communities. They see our closeness to the land, the symbols around here, as an appropriate cultural heart-beat.*(i/v)

The local economy may afford dissimilar and at times disproportionate financial opportunities for its participants. Nonetheless, the economic facet of cultural production is enmeshed in degrees of dependence, especially because the did-jeridu industry is still very much a micro-economic cottage-industry in that individual producers provide many of the didjeridus and recordings, relatively small-scale outlets retail them and social relationships are often established and maintained on a one-to-one basis.

Technological and aesthetic facets

The technological and aesthetic facets of cultural production are influenced by the global flow of technologies of mechanical production and reproduction and by more localised aesthetic considerations. An example of mutual appropriation for Aboriginal and non-Aboriginal musicians, recording engineers and producers is the evolution of what can be termed the 'Aboriginal sound', of which the didjeridu is an integral element. A 'sound' in popular music terminology is comprised of the ephemeral connection between a particular place and the style of recordings made there. Components of a 'sound' include what instrumentation is used; how the music is performed; and, how that performance is sonically manipulated via technology. Most importantly, however, a 'sound' is also socially constructed. It is not the actual 'sound' of a place per se as much as how recorded performances are perceived, mediated and socially reinforced. Having an identifiable 'sound', often associated with a specific geographic locale such as Los Angeles, Manchester or Seattle, is a major requisite for candidature for entry into the'universal pop aesthetic' (Frith, 1989) of sound, sight and senti-ment. Because of the presence of CAAMA's recording studio, Alice Springs is very much at the forefront of the evolution of the 'Aboriginal sound' in Austra-lian popular music and the didjeridu is a readily recognisable ingredient.

As a producer and engineer for CAAMA, Stan Satour deals with a range of technical and aesthetic considerations when using didjeridu. Satour has no hard and fast rules as to presenting it within a recording's soundscape:

> *... everybody has their own view on how they want to go about it. I tend*
> *to lean more towards an 'ambient' sound so you get distance, which gives*
> *me dryness, which to me is this country around Alice Springs.* (i/v)

Musically, Satour prefers 'some kind of pulse beat' and feels there are some
genres of popular music recorded at CAAMA that the didjeridu suits aesthetically
better than others:

> *The dance stuff ... like House ... with the song breathing a lot works well.*
> *It does go well with Techno for some reason ... But Country and Western,*
> *no way. Rock and Roll, it's passable. Ballads, as long as it's here and*
> *there and not overdone; because a lot of people tend to over use didj just*
> *for the sake of the didj player being there ... and to me that's wrong.*
> *Ambient, as in sound-tracks for movies, great. You can't beat having a*
> *didj by itself with a very small reverb. It can create so much space. It's*
> *like looking at a desert picture, it gives you space in the head.* (i/v)

Ross Muir also has extensive experience recording and mixing didjeridu and
concludes that 'one of the problems with the didj in a studio is that it *is* just a
didj in a studio' (i/v). Muir recounts what happened when he and Andrew
Langford tried to record outdoors in the Alice Springs' natural environs:

> *We tried ... to record the actual ambience of the gorge with a stereo mike*
> *at the same time as Andrew's playing. We wanted to forget the digital*
> *reverbs ... but there were so many problems from wind to flies to Andrew*
> *himself just feeling that he couldn't get it together that early in the*
> *morning. We had to go there early morning to get out of the way of*
> *tourists ... We tried so many times and then we just gave up and went*
> *back to his house.* (i/v)

Micaleff offers an opinion on having to adopt or adapt a Western technological
and aesthetic sense in recording and marketing Aboriginal music:

> *... we go back to the band and see what they want to achieve. If they want*
> *to achieve ... mainstream success, then basically like any other producer*
> *would, we will say, for example 'Ok, that's fantastic, but a 32 minute*
> *song won't do'. But a lot of artists are coming in pretty openly willing*
> *to try ... It's difficult to have a winning formula, but I think that Yothu*
> *Yindi has set a bit of a benchmark. There's a dance market, there's a*
> *traditional ambient music market, there's a rock market and any Abo-*
> *riginal artist deserves the right to have access to any one of those.* (i/v)

He argues that world music is 'one of the best options for a young artist' and
suggests how didjeridu music in particular and Aboriginal music and the Abo-

riginal 'sound' in general can be technologically and aesthetically considered a part of world music:

> ... *world music is music ... that blends different instrumentations, but which reflects the local sounds. World music, for me, actually means highly local music well recorded and marketed globally ... What's exciting about Australian music starts in the Northern Territory for a lot of international people ... They don't want to know about our rock bands that can sound like Crowded House or INXS. They want to know what's local.* (i/v)

The technological and aesthetic facets of cultural production inform two primary trends in the development of an Aboriginal 'sound' in and around Alice Springs and elsewhere. One is the incorporation of didjeridu into Aboriginal and non-Aboriginal contemporary performance in genres such as world music. Another is the documentation of traditional Aboriginal performance that may also find an outlet in world music but can also serve less commercial, more cultural agendas.

The media facet

The media facet of cultural production is important because within and through media notions of both Aboriginality and non-Aboriginality are moulded. Consequently, they are influential in the poly-ethnogenesis of the Australian nation-state itself and to attendant discourse(s) of colonialism. Central to this overall process are notions of identity and its concomitant, authenticity; which Clifford (1985) suggests 'cannot be natural or innocent ... [being] tied up with nationalist politics, with restrictive laws and with contested encodations of past and future' (238). In a tourist *entrepôt* such as Alice Springs, the interaction of these processes is further complicated by global flows of information, entertainment and of mass-tourism, where idealised 'impressions' and ersatz 'encounters' have been consciously constructed through expensive and extensive advertising campaigns – advertising campaigns which, like many media representations, only ever reflect by accident the verity beneath the veneer.

I focus here on the remarks of CAAMA's overall media director Owen Cole because of CAAMA's role(s) as a multi-media organisation and retailer of recordings and artifacts. From its broadcast and production facilities in Alice Springs, CAAMA services, via satellite and terrestrial transmitters, a broadcast area which encompasses one third of Australia, at least sixty communities and many outstations. Cole's observations provide an important perspective of media in general and more specifically of indigenous media.

Cole regards CAAMA's mandate to be an encompassing professionalism and asserts that it is 'very important to ensure that we have a high [Aboriginal] content in our programming across the board' (i/v). Didjeridu music is but one of many

114

musical genres CAAMA records and distributes nationally to commercial outlets and other Aboriginal media. Cole comments on this eclecticism:

> *It's really a mirror of what tastes are like in the general society in Australia. I always listen to the request hour and I reckon that's a perfect reflection of it. It goes from evangelistic to heavy metal ... to country and western, to contemporary rock ... and right across to reggae and even some of the young lads who are doing sort of rappish type music.* (i/v)

Cole observes that Aboriginal media and music in particular, have a strong, albeit equivocal, impact in Alice Springs and the central desert region:

> *You just have to be out at the remote communities to see the joy music brings to Aboriginal communities. But quite frankly, the young kids are caught in this real dilemma: they're getting bombarded with all the new communication technologies and it's important that they can become involved and use it in a way that's appropriate for them. Music is just unbelievable to experience out in the communities and to encourage that we need to keep on producing it and we need to use the radio station and make sure that the people ... are hearing their bands.* (i/v)

The Aboriginal music element is crucial to CAAMA and Cole speculates that:

> *If Aboriginal music disappeared completely tomorrow ... I'm going to sound like 150 other radio stations. It's a bit like all the arts and crafts shops in Alice Springs: the real challenge is being different because everyone's jumped on the band wagon, they see dollars in it.* (i/v)

Didjeridu music is an admittedly minor but nonetheless symbolically central facet of cultural production in indigenous media. Having access to CAAMA's state-of-the-art radio, television, recording and marketing facilities has benefit-ted didjeridu music and musicians in three main ways. First, it provides a facility for professional production and marketing. Second, it furnishes an immediate audience; affords artists and communities an opportunity to develop and in some cases preserve, their musical skills and traditions. Third, it supplies a forum for the enunciation of socio-cultural and political agenda.

The interpersonal facet

The interpersonal facet of cultural production is many-sided because it incorporates not only individuals' personalities but also the diverse world views and cultural logics of Aboriginal and non-Aboriginal Australians and tourists from around the world. Notions of ethnicity, often conflated unproblematically with those of race, are an important consideration here because they underscore mass

115

tourism in Alice Springs. Mass tourism itself tends to regard ethnicity and race as romanticised and fixed categories and underplays their socially constructed and dynamic nature. Interpersonal relations in this context are an amalgam of, among other things, the objectification of difference fetishised in Aborigines and Aboriginalia and the subjective experiences of social actors filtered through often contradictory and inconsistent notions of ethnicity and race. It is the latter that I emphasise here, specifically in matters of intra- and inter-cultural etiquette.

An awareness of Aboriginal intra-cultural etiquette helps Satour when he is recording or producing Aboriginal bands. One example is when he feels compelled to dissuade them from using didjeridu in genres where he feels it is not aesthetically appropriate:

> ... the best way's to try .. in a diplomatic way and talk them out of it. I try to steer them away from using didjeridu in a really, really nice way. One thing about Aboriginal people, you tell them something straight out and they tend to take it as an offensive thing, but there are other ways of doing things and getting them to see both pictures nice and evenly. (i/v)

Nickolls observes that the main buyers of didjeridus are predominantly non-Australian males and outlines a general national profile of customers he has encountered:

> A lot of Germans and other Europeans, Americans as well, like to buy it. Not too many Asian people really and when they do they don't really buy it to play it, it's more ornamental. But the Europeans mainly get right into it and go for it and that's why I've had the accompanying information translated into German, French and Italian. (i/v)

A contentious aspect of intra- and inter-cultural etiquette that garners considerable comment is that of women buying or playing didjeridu because some Aborigines and non-Aborigines regard it as an exclusively male instrument. Langford engages with this issue by providing relevant information and letting tourists make up their own minds:

> A lot [of non-Aboriginal women] are aware or have heard that traditional Aboriginal women don't play and [consequently] they are not sure whether they should play it or not. I just say, 'Look, traditionally Aboriginal ladies don't play it, but the men I've spoken to don't mind European women playing it.' [But] it is a men's ceremonial instrument'. Then people just sort of work it through, work out whether they want to try and pick it up or not. (i/v)

Nickolls comments on the specific case of the involvement of non-Aborigines using the didjeridu in 'New Age' social/ spiritual activities:

116

... they actually came out here before and held a 'New Age' corroboree with the Pitjantjatjara women. They want to create this new Dreaming ... where we're all combined. There was a bloke who has been in Alice Springs selling didjeridus, he's just gone down to Melbourne to one of those shaman things ... and he is going to teach them all how to play didj. He teaches any woman to play ... He sees it that everyone should be able to play and that the Aboriginal people haven't got exclusivity over it, which I disagree with. (i/v)

Even though Nickolls has his own opinion on the issue of exclusivity, he acknowledges it is not cut and dried:

I don't totally disagree about exclusivity, but I just think some non-Aboriginal people should respect that playing in front of some Aboriginal people may offend them. If you want to do it in private, in your own home, there's no one going to stop you doing that. (i/v)

The interpersonal facet of cultural production is a site where numerous aspects of the didjeridu in the desert converge, such as the matter of intra- and inter-cultural etiquette. These are many-sided because of the didjeridu's significance as an ethnically and racially identified musical instrument; its roles in the iconography, symbolism and political economy of Aboriginality; and, its ubiquity as a commodity whose networks of cultural production encompass people from diverse heritages.

The ideological facet

The ideological facet of cultural production is omnipresent. It is influenced by an idealised and often inconsistent and inchoate, feature of many liberal-democratic nation-states: supposed equality of fair treatment and life chances for their indigenous peoples. This gets played out contradictorily in Australia's local, national and international political arenas in part because of the mythology of it being a country where everyone gets a 'fair-go', a fiction formally enshrined and repeatedly trumpeted in governments' assertions of freedom, democracy and human rights for all. However, the demonstrable inequality of access to fair treatment and life chances for Aborigines across Australia is also present in Alice Springs and the central desert region. Ideology impacts implicitly or explicitly on several levels: institutional and individual racism; the issue of appropriation, in the sense of making some thing one's own; and the politicisation of the didjeridu.

Micaleff comments that CAAMA's efforts to develop experienced, well-rounded musicians has run into instances where local attitudes and practices do not mirror official policies concerning 'a fair-go':

> *Alice Springs is a unique kind of a place. But unfortunately racism still does exist, with venue bookers in particular getting nervous about booking Aboriginal bands because, 'Oh my God, then Aboriginal people might actually come here' ... A lot of Aboriginal people haven't had the opportunity to perform because of that racism and to get involved in the music industry. But here in Alice Springs a certain level of balance has been struck and I think that a lot of local Aboriginal people appreciate CAAMA being here tremendously because we can build those bridges.* (i/v)

Nickolls has done freelance performance in schools in Alice Springs and elsewhere, which can have undercurrents of racism:

> *Some schools are better than others, of course. Some schools they just call out 'nigger' and 'coon' and 'boong' and all this shit ... Those are mainly high schools, but the primary school kids haven't got much of that racism and so they're pretty open. Most teachers are pretty good, but I have had some who have just whinged to me ... But I don't go to ... represent the whole Aboriginal race and I don't have to cop every little gripe they've got. I get a bit of 'Are you a 'real' Aborigine?'. But I don't force [my identity] down people's throats, if they don't want to accept it ... that's their bad luck, it's no great loss for me.* (i/v)

At another ideological level, Nickolls notes that there is a circuit of overtly politicised gigs available for a didjeridu performer such as 'government functions ... and all the ethnic festivals'. At these, Nickolls finds different levels of politicisation:

> *Some people would totally ignore the politics and not want to have anything to do with it. And with some people, you'd rock up and someone is trying to make a political statement, having a didj player and all that stuff. I'm a political person myself and I don't mind that, but sometimes the didj is a bit removed from that and to communicate with people you have to leave that a bit alone, because sometimes the didjeridu music is the first Aboriginal things that are going on.* (i/v)

Micaleff touches upon an ideological aspect that has socio-cultural and political undercurrents: appropriation. Issues of appropriation have particular resonance for Aborigines because of their impact on efforts to exert influence on representations and gain recognition within the politics of culture.

> *I was at the Alice Springs' airport and came across a cassette which I don't mind naming ... called* Moods of the Didjeridu. *It had no standard copyright protection clauses on it, it had no information about the artists.*

> *There was three paragraphs of lots of motherhood-type language about how wonderful the sound of a didjeridu is and that it represents Aboriginality and the oldest culture in the world, etc. But it's quite likely that from what I know of every active Aboriginal musician in the country, they would certainly be proudly putting their name on it [if they produced it]. It certainly would be copyright registered, this wasn't. It's highly likely to be not an 'authentic' product, but it's still selling for $29 and someone's buying it, just because of demand.* (i/v)

This incident raises the issue of appropriation as it impacts on CAAMA as a producer and marketer of didjeridu music:

> *... there's quite a strong market for didjeridu music but at CAAMA we're very careful and* Moods of the Didjeridu *makes us very angry, because it really is cultural theft. The didjeridu is an instrument that belongs to the world, but it is a product that obviously is a bit dubious.* (i/v)

Appropriation also has a surreal side. Micaleff says:

> *... some of us really laugh when we see some white-fellas playing didj who just don't tune it. People add didj to make it sound Aboriginal, but we actually find it quite humorous. Can you imagine how funny it would sound to us for someone to pick up the Spanish guitar and start playing ... with all the strings upside down and totally de-tuned?* (i/v)

The ideological facet of cultural production impacts profoundly not only on social relationships between Aborigines and non-Aborigines but also enables some level of agency on the part of Aborigines to affect change in asymmetrical power-knowledge relations with the dominant culture. Aboriginal popular songs often articulate what are in essence ideological concerns and the didjeridu can function as aural ideology.

Conclusion

If we pull back from the theoretical and ethnographical prisms we have been using and take a wider and less analytical view, like that afforded a tourist flying out of Alice Springs, we would see a relatively obscure musical instrument previously used only by small groups of people quite suddenly being made in large quantities and sold to total strangers in an isolated place. Why? Is it commodity fetishism? The mingling of mass tourism, mass consumption and musical exotica? The aesthetisation of national icons? The theft of a sound (and a soul?) to relieve an attack of aesthetic ennui on post-modern (wo)man? Probably a bit of all of the above given the diversity of social actors, agendas and alliances involved.

The ethnographic data illustrates some of the paradoxes and complexities of the didjeridu's cultural production in and around Alice Springs, a place where the transnational flows of the global cultural economy converge, refract and mutate as they interact with mass tourism and with notions of contemporary indigeneity, Aboriginality and the Australian nation-state. In some contexts commerce may seem to take precedence and in others culture may seem to do so, but they are mostly quite inseparable.

The didjeridu in the desert acquires meaningfulness as an object when situated in systems of symbols, values and exchange. It may be not be what it was made to be (a musical instrument of Aboriginal culture) but rather what it has come to be (the nexus of complex social relations and an ethnographic object entangled in culture and commerce). It may well be that for many tourists and others, the didjeridu is an aural and material memento, evidence of a cultural encounter. However, for some indigenous peoples in Australia it is much more. Even if mass tourism were to cease, the didjeridu is likely to retain a vital and evolving role.[13] As Art Nicholls observes:

> *There are many Aboriginal people like me who have lost a lot of the culture. The didjeridu is something that we know that we've got, so we're going to hold on strongly.* (i/v)

Acknowledgements: Thanks to the informants, Guy Grant, Paul Scott, Australia Post Staff and anonymous reviewers for their input.

Notes

1. CAAMA is not the focus here but needs to be appreciated as an important, unique and at times controversial indigenous media institution. See Ginsburg (1993), Michaels (1994), Meadows (1994) and Molnar (1994) for discussions of indigenous media in Australia.

2. For specific examinations of Aboriginalia see Jones (1992 a+b) and Pearson (1991). On Australian Aboriginal arts and crafts see Altman (1989), Sutton (1988) and Ioannou (1992).

3. 'The Alice' began as a telegraph station and has grown into the main population centre for the vast Central Desert region. It is an administration and business hub and access point for the major tourist destinations of Uluru (Ayers Rock), Kata Tjuta (The Olgas) and Kings Canyon. It is also the symbolic centre of the 'The Outback', an amorphous term for the vast, thinly populated but resource rich interior areas of Australia. 'Aboriginal Australia' is an vague term given the diverse living conditions and aspiration of Aborigines. See Fourmile (1994) for an Aboriginal perspective on indigenous arts in the contexts of Australian multiculturalism and national identity.

4. There is a sizeable literature on Aboriginal musical traditions in the Central Desert region, for example Ellis (1964; 1985) on Pitjantjatjara music. The didjeridu has recently been incorporated into some popular music ensembles in the region.

5. Michaels (1994) raises the issue of 'bad' Aboriginal art, which is germane here given that the overall quality and playability of tourist market didjeridus varies considerably with no firm criteria as to what constitutes a 'good' one either as art or instrument.

6.   See Myers (1994 and 1991) for useful discussions of representations of Australian Aboriginal culture via artistic expression and Michaels (1994) on its commoditisation.

7.   Appadurai (1986) also proposes that a thing can have a 'career' (a trajectory and a history) which often entails mutating roles as a commodity.

8.   In 1993/94 a total of 494,000 interstate and overseas tourists visited the Northern Territory. Approximately 25 per cent of overseas visitors and 9 per cent of interstate visitors identified the purchase of Aboriginalia as their main activity and interest – Northern Territory Tourist Commission(1994).

9.   Bourdieu (1993) defines the general field of cultural production within which things are created and circulated as 'the system of objective relations ... functionally defined by their role in the division of labour of production, reproduction and diffusion' (115). In the limited context of artworks, Jensen (1990) defines cultural production as 'the manifestation of interacting beliefs, policies and practices rather than as the linear creation of particular consumer objects'(11). Frith (1992) suggests that the perspective of producers tends to be under-emphasised in analyses of popular music.

10.   See Neuenfeldt for discussions, respectively, of the didjeridu in world music (1994) and technologisation and cultural transposition (1993).

11.   Becker (1982) provides a comprehensive and accessible analysis of the complexity of art worlds and art-works.

12.   Conversation with the author, 1994.

13.   The following example demonstrate the ubiquity of the didjeridu in contemporary Australian culture. For the 1995 visit of Pope John Paul II a headline in the *West Australian* read 'Didjeridus Herald Arrival' and went on to note: 'The ceremony began with didjeridus amplified through speakers and the Aboriginal flag projected on two big screens either side of the crowd' (unattributed 1995: 8).

Bibliography

Altman J. (1989) *The Aboriginal Arts and Crafts Industry: Report of the Review Committee*, Canberra: Australian Government Publishing Service.

Appadurai A. (1986) (Introduction to) Appadurai, A (ed) *The Social Life of Things: Commodities in Cultural Perspective*, Sydney: Cambridge University Press.

Appadurai A. (1990) 'Disjuncture and Difference in the Global Cultural Economy', *Public Culture* v2 n2.

Attwood B. and Arnold J. (eds) (1992) *Power, Knowledge and Aborigines*, Melbourne: La Trobe University Press.

Becker H. (1982) *Art Worlds*, Berkeley: University of California Press.

Bourdieu P. (1993) *The Field of Cultural Production*, London: Polity Press.

Clifford D. (1985) 'Objects and Selves – An Afterword' in Stocking, G (ed) *Objects and Others: Essays on Museums and Material Culture*, Madison: University of Wisconsin Press.

Ellis C. (1964) *Aboriginal Music Making: A Study of Central Australian Music*, Adelaide: Libraries Board of South Australia.

Ellis C. (1985) *Aboriginal Music: Education for Living*, Brisbane: University of Queensland Press.

Fourmile H. (1994) 'Aboriginal Arts in Relation to Multiculturalism' in Gunew, S (ed) (1994) *Culture, Difference and the Arts*, Sydney: Allen and Unwin.

Frith S. (1989) *World Music, Politics and Social Change*, New York: Manchester University Press.

Frith S. (1992) 'The Cultural Study of Popular Music' in Grossberg, L Nelson, C and Treichler, P (eds) (1994) *Cultural Studies* London: Routledge.

Ginsburg F. (1991) 'Indigenous Media: Faustian Contract or Global Villages?', *Cultural Anthropology* v16 n1.

Ginsburg F. (1994) 'Embedded Aesthetics: Creating a Discursive Space for Indigenous Media', *Cultural Anthropology* v9n3

Hiller S. (ed) (1991) *The Myth of Primitivism*, London: Routledge.

Ioannou N. (ed) (1992) *Craft in Society: An Anthology of Perspectives*, Fremantle, Australia:Fremantle Arts Centre Press.

Jensen J. (1990) 'Technology/Music: Understanding Processual Relations', *Popular Music and Society* v14 n1.

Jones P. (1992a) 'Arts and Manufacturers: Inventing Aboriginal Craft' in Ioannou, N (ed).

Jones P. (1992b) 'The Boomerang's Erratic Flight: The Mutability of Ethnographic Objects' in Attwood, B and Arnold, J (eds) (1992)

Meadows M. (1992) *A Watering Can in the Desert: The Australian Government Response to Claims for Indigenous Broadcasting Rights*, Brisbane: Institute of Cultural Policy Studies, Griffith University.

Michaels E. (1994) *Bad Aboriginal Art*, Sydney: Allen and Unwin.

Molnar H. (1994) 'Indigenous Media Development in Australia: A Product of Struggle and Opposition', *Cultural Studies* v9 n1.

Moyle A. (1981) 'The Australian Didjeridoo: A Late Musical Intrusion', *World Archaeology* v12.

Myers F. (1991) 'Representing Culture: The Production of Discourse(s) for Aboriginal Acrylic Painting', *Cultural Anthropology* v6 n1.

Myers F. (1994) 'Culture Making at the Asia Society Gallery' *American Ethnologist*, v21 n4.

Neuenfeldt K. (1993) 'The Didjeridu and the Overdub', *Perfect Beat* v1 n2.

Neuenfeldt K. (1994) 'The Cultural Production and Use of the Didjeridu in World Music', *Perfect Beat* v2 n1.

Northern Territory Tourist Commission (1994) *Northern Territory Travel Monitor*, Darwin: Kinhill, Cameron and McNamara.

Pearson C. (1991) 'Aboriginal Representation and Kitsch', in Hiller, S (ed).

Sutton P. (1988) *Dreamings: The Art of Aboriginal Australia*, New York: Viking.

Taussig M. (1992) *The Nervous System*, London: Routledge.

Thomas N. (1991) *Entangled Objects: Exchange, Material Culture and Colonialism in the Pacific*, London: Harvard University Press.

Unattributed (1995a) (untitled)*The Advertiser* (Adelaide) 1/2.

Chapter Eight

TERRA INCOGNITA:

The Career of Charlie McMahon

SHANE HOMAN

Introduction

O ver the last twenty years, the didjeridu has come to constitute an artefact of Aboriginality and has become a familiar motif in the construction and representation of a pan-Aboriginal culture. As a readily identifiable symbol of indigeneity the didjeridu has also been enthusiastically adopted within the labyrinth of musical cross-cultural fusions known as world music. The most commercially successful adaptation of the didjeridu within world music, has of course taken place with the Yolngu band Yothu Yindi's fusion of traditional Arnhem Land sounds and vocals with a standard western bass/guitar/drums/keyboard rock context. The didjeridu is central to the sound and 'both ways' [1] philosophy of the band, in both an aesthetic and political sense. As with its other uses by bands and solo performers, the didjeridu is a signifier of 'site as text' (Collins, 1989: 229) – it evokes a fundamental connection to the particularity of place, to the land as the primary text of everyday life.

Issues concerning the didjeridu and the context of its uses played a significant part in the extended debate over the commercially successful dance remix of Yothu Yindi's *Treaty* single and video and arguments as to whether the remix constituted a subsequent dilution of the song's political agenda.[2] The debate underlined the fact that the use of indigenous instruments and traditions within the world music context can be seen as a highly politicised activity. If Yothu Yindi's own use of the didjeridu (and clap sticks) can be seen as problematic, there are obvious implications for non-Aboriginal uses of the didjeridu – even those which are free of a distinct agenda of indigenous politics and obviously incapable of being tied to a particularity of place.

Over the last decade, the didjeridu has come to be used in increasingly disparate ways in various international contexts. This dispersal of use has been accompanied by attempts to reconcile the use of an instrument defining 'Aboriginalism' with non-Aboriginal or non-traditional usage.[3] In discussing the political aspects of the use and/or appropriation of the instrument by non-traditional groups, this chapter focuses on the work of (Australian, Anglo-Celtic performer) Charlie McMahon, whose career represents a personalised history of the development of the instrument within the wider discourses of world music, Australianness, authenticity and appropriation.

(Note: all quotations attributed to McMahon in this chapter are, unless otherwise specified, taken from interviews with the author conducted in March 1996).

Prefiguring the World Music Genre

As a four year old intrigued by the Charles Chauvel film *Jedda* (1955), McMahon began experimenting with his mother's vacuum cleaner and water pipes, attempting to capture a didjeridu sound. Attempts to learn the didjeridu, however, did not begin seriously until later:

> *Around seventeen or eighteen, the didjeridu was just part of that whole Aboriginal experience ... I felt very good about the naturalness and ease of Aboriginals' appreciation of the bush. But the first lot of blowing I did was with guitars and drums at casual parties, doing stuff like* [the North American group] *The Band. That's when I became aware of tuning. Most people would praise it and say 'Hey, that's good, keep it going'. Sometimes we'd play for hours and hours, this would have been late 1960s. I started playing piano ... the music classes in school were a joke, but I was told that I was getting quite good on piano. I blew my* [right] *hand off shortly after that* [experimenting with rockets] *and I figured I wouldn't be much use in the manual world ... I ended up getting a scholarship and going to Sydney University. At that time I would have picked up my first wooden didj. There used to be an old mission type place near Central Railway station where Charlie Perkins* [and other Aboriginal activists] *used to work. It was the only shop with didjeridus and artefacts. I had that one until someone dropped it on a concrete floor.*

On the strength of his work in the late 1960s and early 1970s, McMahon can lay claim to have been the first non-Aboriginal musician to introduce the didjeridu drone within a rock context. At this stage McMahon believed the didjeridu functioned in a similar capacity to later uses of the synthesiser, in being a multi-layered instrument:

> *I realised that it was a cross between a bass* [guitar] *and a drum and could sit really easy ... to be a bed for the other stuff ... the 'groove generator' for want of a better word. It sets the timing, the tempo, the pitch; and the mood. That's quite a few things for a single instrument. When I say mood, I mean that you can play it up, or play it dark. In that sense the 'du could project that in a way that synthesisers did later.*

Within an amplified rock band context, McMahon increasingly focused on the more technical applications of the instrument. This centred on the importance of endurance, rhythm and the complexities of proper breathing:

> *I think the next stage I would have taken it to was learning a little bit more ...* [making it more] *complex. By 1975 I'd already figured how to play in a groove for half an hour and tune it to A440 tuning. So the next thing was to learn different rhythm textures and ways of breathing; so when you breathed in, you could do a half breath. It adds to the complexity and is the key to it I think. You can then break it up and do all sorts of things. If you can breath half breaths, it means you can start using 99 breaths a minute. 99 is quite an easy one to play; so with 4 beats every bar, you get 3 breaths. That put me in a position to play in a rock context.*

After completing an arts and town-planning degree at Sydney University, McMahon tutored in town-planning at the university until dismissed as a result of differences with the vice chancellor. He then spent four years on the south coast of New South Wales doing labouring work. In 1978 he accepted a job as Development Coordinator for the Kintore and Kiwirrkurra areas in the Western Desert region of central Australia. He oversaw the supervision of the Federal Department of Aboriginal Affairs' grants to the out stations around Papunya, some of which were 100 kilometres away from each other. After a year and a half, McMahon left the job to tour with Midnight Oil. He recalls being amazed 'how good a didj could sound through a good PA [amplification system]' since 'before that I might have played through 80 watt amplifiers', whereas Midnight Oil 'had 5000 watts a side'.

In 1980 McMahon played with a number of musicians in North America, including Jerry Garcia (from the Grateful Dead) and Mark Isham (from Van Morrison's band) and performed as support on a Timothy Leary lecture tour. He recalls that North American audiences were appreciative once their singular preconceptions of the didjeridu were removed:

125

Charlie McMahon (1994).

The only thing they knew was Tie Me Kangaroo Down [by Rolf Harris], *which was ok in a way, but it was a stereotyped characterisation. So over there I started calling it a yi<u>d</u>aki ... I mainly found them very cultural minded. Some of the redneck places found it very strange; some didn't even realise that Australia had an indigenous population.*

Gondwanaland

Upon his return to Australia, McMahon conceived the idea of forming a band comprising didjeridu, synthesisers and percussion. Gondwanaland was formed in 1981 when he linked up with synthesiser player Peter Carolan. They played a number of concerts but their progress was interrupted when McMahon was asked to return to Kintore to establish water bores in some of the outlying stations (critical to the survival of Pintubi wishing to live in the more remote areas of the Western Desert region). It was in this work that McMahon realised the centrality of the land to the indigenous population as the symbolic site of power and practice:

> *I didn't play the didj, except when I was in town. It wasn't part of the tradition up there, nowhere near it. They really believe in singing, that if you sing to your country, it'll hear it. They don't perform any cor-roborees as entertainment. In the first three years there, there was not one death, although we did a few emergency evacuations by Flying Doctor. You could see how the spiritual connectedness to the land had given the people clarity and strength. I learnt a lot about bush practice, food. I didn't really get involved with the ceremonial stuff, although I was often taken to them. Nor did I enquire much about it, because it was their beliefs and I didn't really believe in the same way. I've had too much science bunged into me, that's part of it ... I couldn't see that it would do anything for me. For what I was doing, I didn't want my involvement* [in ceremonies] *to become an issue.*

Gondwanaland's first recording, *Terra Incognita* ('land unknown')[4], was made in 1982. The recording represents the beginning of McMahon's effort to capture the surroundings he had worked in: an aural documentation of 'soundscapes for landscapes'.[5] The tracks were augmented by guitar and violin, provided by Andrew de Teliga and occasional drum rhythms, supplied by Rob Hirst of Midnight Oil. With the success of the album and live work, McMahon left his desert job to concentrate on his family, establishing the band and session work.

McMahon has worked often with Midnight Oil and was a guide and musician on their 1986 'Black Fella White Fella' tour of Central Australia. In describing their series of albums, *Dead Heart* (1986), *Diesel and Dust* (1988) and *Blue Sky Mining* (1990), Rob Hirst has stated that with Midnight Oil 'the sense of our music is space ... absorbing the great open space of Australia and putting it down in a musical form' (cited O'Donnell, 1991: 55). Within different contexts and practicalities, Hirst's comments can also be applied to Gondwanaland's sound. McMahon's work entails an aural bibliography of his travels. The notion of travel is an important theme in investigating unexplored (musical and geographical) territory[6]. In negotiating the specificity of Western Desert landscapes, McMahon constructs musical soundscapes which attempt to capture 'the part that derives from the land and that's the freedom, the brightness of it'. Popular music may provide new ways of negotiating spaces and states (Murphie, 1996: 18) and McMahon's use of the didjeridu derives in part from a desire to find new ways of thinking about the relations between site, sound and text. Whereas Yothu Yindi's music, for example, is underlined by a more politicised affiliation and faith in the land as the basis for existence within Aboriginal culture, McMahon's music evokes a more unspecified connection to the land, preferring to let '[audiences'] imaginations ride ... I like the music to have a certain amount of obscurity to leave enough for the imagination for people to find their own thing in it'.

Given the aesthetic and aural composition of the recordings and the band itself, the mainstream music industry has experienced its usual difficulty in placing Gondwanaland within a suitable marketing category and style. Their music has been categorised across a range of generic styles: tribal, rock, folk, jazz, classical, country, indigenous and atmospheric. The absence of vocals has confused the mainstream industry, accustomed as it is to the standard bass/drums/guitar/keyboard/vocals line-up:

> *We did cop some criticism, some people thought we were too melodic, there was the ambient side to it. At that time the emphasis was on bright tongue-in-cheek melodies à la* [Queen's lead vocalist] *Freddie Mercury ... there was a harder attitude. People couldn't connect to the different kind of energy. We were halfway between an art band and a rock band. But we've found our own niche and our own places. But it did really disappoint me that we were doing really experimental music and we've never been able to get any Australia Council funding.*

The band has proven popular with film makers seeking aural images of Australian landscapes. McMahon's didjeridu has been used within a wide range of thematic projects, from the commercial (*Mad Max – Beyond Thunderdome, Until The End Of The World*), the educational (*The Drifting Museum*) to the political (*Koori: A Will To Win*). In constructing film soundtracks which require aural spatial images of the bush, McMahon believes 'the didj is excellent, because you lock into a nice rhythm and it's so easy to hold that to a story'.

Technique

As a player of some thirty years standing, McMahon is acknowledged within both Aboriginal and non-Aboriginal communities as one of the most technically accomplished in the world. He believes constant experimentation with breathing techniques to be the key to endurance and a distinctive style:

People tell me my style – if it's known for anything – is known for [its]
*rapid breathing ... It produces much clearer and stronger overtones ... I
don't know of many people that play with the same amount of rhythmic
complexity.*

McMahon's approach to didjeridu playing is based on its use in an ensemble
context and aesthetic, where he emphasises that:

*Because I've been part of a group, I know my place. A lot of 'du players
that I have worked with, they tend to want to break out on their own.
Basically you've got to settle down into a steady groove; it is naturally
a drone instrument ...* [For example,] *I see a lot of people these days,
they'll do a reggae thing and the didj will come in* [later]. *What I like to
think in the stuff I've done is that we start with the didj as the essential
groove. It's not a feature so much, but the essential ingredient in the
arrangement.*

In this sense the didjeridu acts as the fundamental 'bed' for percussion and
synthesiser interactions. Yet the most distinctive feature of Gondwanaland's
recordings lies in the 'rhythmic complexity' of McMahon's didjeridu playing,
where the foundational drone is often accentuated by overlapping multi-tonal
splashes and interjections.

Gondwanaland's arrangements are sparse in comparison to a number of bands
who have pursued a multi-layered approach in utilising the didjeridu in their
instrumental line-up.[7] Gondwanaland officially disbanded in 1992 and McMahon's 1994 album *Travelling Songs* was released under the truncated group name
of Gondwana. On this album McMahon adopted a more multi-instrumental style
and engaged in a wider interplay with other musicians and writers, notably
Arnhem Land Aboriginal singer/songwriter Bobby Bunuggurr. The album also
showcased the use of McMahon's 'chromatic rack', a set of twelve differently
pitched didjeridus which alleviates tuning difficulties:

*'Du players are the people probably most disrespectful of tunings. Often
it'll be a random process. Most traditional 'dus are cut short because
the higher pitch is louder. That's why I'll have a range of 'dus from C
and below. In traditional use there's not much use for anything below
(D). D# is my lowest.*

McMahon has found another method of extending the didj's range. He has
developed an instrument, which he calls the 'didjeribone', which slides a smaller
pipe within a larger didj.[8] The variable length of this invention has created a
multi-tonic instrument, particularly useful for live performances. As he emphasises, the instrument gives him 'another two octaves to play with'. His latest
(1996) recording *Tjilatjila* (a term for slow and gentle movement in Western

Desert language) is perhaps the best example of the complexities of McMahon's style, where different breathing patterns and the use of multi-tonic didjs produce a pan pipe-ish or trumpet-like effect ('didj horns'). Accompanied by strings and piano, much greater melodic emphasis is placed with the multi-layered effects of the didj. It is the tonal possibilities of the instrument which currently excite McMahon:

> *I'll often hear things, melodies and you go to do them on piano and you can't. There are things that you can do where you can sing an overtone over the drone. It's amazing and it's a bit like a voice. I'm looking at the theories of soundwaves and extending the range.*

McMahon has resisted commercial pressures to place the band's style more forcefully within the more superficial exotica of the world music genre. It has been suggested on more than one occasion that McMahon was not marketing himself in the 'best' light:

> *A lot of people have said that I should do the whole bit, with body paint. The record companies often suggest that too. I had one guy tell me: 'Charlie, you could go all the way, be as big as* [Australian pop singer] *Johnny Farnham, but what you need is a black sheila* [Aboriginal women] *with good tits and the face paint and you'll be off'.*

Such remarks heighten the perception that the mainstream recording industry is only too willing to reinforce irrelevant (and culturally ignorant) marketing stereotypes in return for commercial success. While McMahon's live appearances embody a unique style and performance aesthetic – as vigorous visually as it is musically – it seems that audiences and those within the industry attempt to project their own agendas onto the music.

A number of other western discourses have been imposed upon the didjeridu. These have often combined the instrument's traditional 'mystical' attachment to land and place with an assortment of enigmatic cultural contexts and associations. As Fiona Magowan discusses in Chapter 11 of this anthology, in the international context the didjeridu has been implicated within a set of discourses relating to spirituality and self-healing. The claims of such inherent properties of didjeridu playing are not new and represent further examples of cultural appropriation removed from its original contexts. In his comprehensive examination of the mimetic discourses of colonialism, Taussig (1995) refers to the ways in which colonialist forces often imitate indigenous cultures as a powerful weapon over the colonised, 'the power of the copy to influence what it is a copy of' (250). In discussing the instances where such imitations occurred, Taussig develops the notion of 'sympathetic magic', where 'the magician [colonialist] infers that he can produce any effect he desires merely by imitating it' (ibid: 47).

This translates as an effective description of those didjeridu players who seek or make claims of the transcendental properties of the instrument. As a musician with more legitimate claims than most to use of the instrument in relation to 'authentic' spiritual connections, McMahon is clearly aware of the contradictions of such assertions:

> *Look, I don't care what people do with it. The only thing I find funny and strange in 'du playing and objectionable, are people who make enormous claims to some mysterious themes of the Dreamtime; that by playing this thing they're going to be spiritually grounded. That stuff just cracks me up ... I do know it's incredibly good for your health. I haven't had a cold since 1983 and I put a lot of that down to the fact that 'du playing really teaches you to breathe. It does, I think, slow your heart rate and makes you breathe more efficiently. But so far as those other claims, that's where I draw the line. I don't go and plagiarise that Dreamtime stuff and I think the people who are essentially out there, they should just say they're there to play and try and sell some records, just get on with it and have a good time and stop all this claptrap about spirituality.*

The notion that the spiritual aspects and ambience of the didjeridu can be achieved outside the ritual contexts of Aboriginal ceremony is one of the more disturbing by-products of its use in world music. Such essentialistic associations ignore (and distort) a range of underlying contextual meanings. At its worst, such claims to an earthly spirituality derive from blatant commercial opportunism.[9] In this sense didjeridu mythologies are appropriated as important marketing tools. For non-Aboriginal players, perhaps the mythologies have become so powerful that it is widely believed that one *can't* play without evoking and engaging a deeper state of consciousness. Such mythologies have become embedded in the performance meanings associated with the instrument.

Tjilatjila: **From apathy to acceptance**

The relatively recent inclusion of the didjeridu into the repertoire of New Age mysticism (and western impressions of Dreamtime spirituality) has affected a change in the status of the instrument. It is no longer just an object of anthropological fascination. Audience reactions throughout McMahon's career indicate the changing perceptions to uses of the didjeridu outside traditional ritual contexts. Such changes in attitude relate directly to changes in perceptions of the validity of Aboriginal culture. In the late 1960s, McMahon, as a non-Aboriginal didjeridu player, challenged Eurocentric notions of cultural superiority and racism:

> *There was an attitude to learning the didj from* [non-Aboriginal] *people*

131

of 'why bother?' The sort of people who said that were fools ... I have been at gigs where people have said 'Oh, you're playing black, coon songs'. I've actually had that comment said to me over the years.

With Gondwanaland's commercial successes and the demand locally and internationally for his current live projects, McMahon has witnessed the transformation in the commercial and aesthetic reception of his recordings and performances. Audience reaction in the 1990s now largely consists of a preoccupation with technique and sounds, although the wider discourses of significationtion remain, 'especially live, people will ask me what I imagine while I'm playing; they think you're on a spiritual journey every time you pick it up and play'. The shift in audience reactions, away from a sense of cultural apathy (or open hostility) to more practical terms of engagement and enquiry, suggests a more fundamental change in a contextual perspective of the didjeridu, rather than any significant changes in McMahon's style. The commercial success of Gondwanaland represented industrial and audience acceptance of McMahon's fusion aesthetic which he had been practising since the 1960s.

Within an Australian context, Gondwanaland has revealed the possibilities of the didjeridu within world music, specifically the fusion of didjeridu sounds with intricate percussion and synthesiser to produce a 'Euro-ambient' style (Mitchell, 1996: 209). McMahon can lay claim to being one of the first to realise the potential of the instrument outside the boundaries of Aboriginal ritual performance:

> *It became interesting in the mid-1980s, when Aboriginal culture became 'Number 1 mate!', it was funny to see that happen ... [To] booking agencies like Nucleus, at first it was a joke. They couldn't even say the [band's] name. It was really hard for them to put us in a category.*

White man/black instrument

In being acknowledged as an innovator, McMahon has continually stressed the experimental nature of his music, the ability to place didjeridu sounds within new rhythmical and instrumental contexts, free of more elaborate connections to 'authentic' Aboriginal reference points. It is this consistent awareness that traditional Aboriginal styles cannot be appropriated for commercial use, which McMahon believes enables him to enjoy good working relations with Aboriginal didjeridu performers and audiences:

> *I get on pretty good with traditional didj players ... I play with Mark Atkins a fair bit. I think it's great that the race relations aren't so bad that I can do what I do. The reason why I've got such a good relation with the traditional people is that I don't plagiarise. Also, because I'm*

into it quite heavily, I'm more popular. I do get a few Koori [South Eastern Australian Aboriginal] *guys who ask me 'How do you play that wobble* [riff]*?'*.

Certainly, the extensive time McMahon spent working with Aboriginal communities in the Western Desert region has produced a mutual respect based on implicit assumptions that some musical and cultural experiences cannot be shared.[10]

Perhaps the more innovative aspect of McMahon's career lies in the way in which Gondwanaland has been one of the bands involved in challenging and redefining past industry perceptions of what constitutes a distinctively Australian music. As experiences with booking agencies of the 1970s (such as Nucleus) reveal, the conservative non-Aboriginal mainstream industry was not prepared to accept performers and musics outside the strict confines of the guitar-based axis of the Oz rock tradition. Similarly, the band's 'soundscapes for landscapes' approach challenged the master narrative of Australian pop mythology which evokes images of white suburban or inner city traditions of rebellion.

The 'authentic' margins within the context of popular music it seems, are only truly authentic if viewed as marginal in an obvious sense, geographically or culturally. In terms of authenticity, McMahon has suffered a type of 'reverse essentialism' from venues and audiences who expect Aboriginal didjeridu performers:

I've noticed it with a few people. I've had jobs and turned up and people have been surprised when they see a white-fella. They're disappointed and sometimes they'll ask for a 'dinky-di' [i.e. 'genuine'] *didj player and sometimes I'll bring some Koori guys along to play. That's the thing, it's not the sound, but the whole cultural context to them.*

The desire for the presence of Aboriginal musicians in order to produce 'dinky-di' performances constitutes a reversal of past racist industry practices which actively discouraged Aboriginal bands on the Australian pub circuit.[11] Such experiences reveal the difficulties in separating the practices of didjeridu playing from associated stereotyped cultural discourses. In the eyes of some audiences, McMahon has suffered from not meeting the essential(istic) criteria for 'serious' study of the instrument, in that he is not an Aborigine who (in the best world music stereotype 'tradition') derives from the authentic isolation of Arnhem Land or elsewhere in northern Australia. The time McMahon spent working in the Western Desert region has undoubtedly helped in an (unconscious) effort to meet the cruder notions of 'authenticity'. On a broader level, his work there emphasised to him the importance of place to local Aboriginal peoples in symbolising self-determination, security and possession of the self. It is instruc-

133

tive to note that issues of legitimacy have, with one exception,[12] not been raised by Aboriginal players or audiences:

> *Most* [non-Aboriginal] *people have the wrong idea. The most common question I get asked by a journo* [journalist] *is what Aboriginals think of my playing ... There's a huge awareness in this country of racial shame and we have to bore our way through it. It's not being perpetrated now so much as it was ... Most people, whatever their perceptions, I find are terribly poorly informed. After my work and living in various places, I think I'm fairly well informed about various issues. On that whole issue of cultural propriety, I think I'm ok.*

One result of the association of the didjeridu with essentialistic qualities of spirituality and a New Age other-worldness has been a particular perception of Aboriginal culture and its essential difference by non-Aboriginal communities. This perception is one which cannot accommodate the image of a non-Aboriginal didjeridu player without confronting issues of cultural guilt or wrongdoing. In his discussion of the reception of Aboriginal rock and the discursive minefield of 'white/black' musical contact, Castles (1993) produces a characterisation which can be applied to McMahon's situation:

> *The pleasure of allowing the music to sink in and take on ambient meaning in the midst of your own life, on which popular music depends, is immediately intercepted by anxiety about the 'cultural prejudices' of your interpretation ... Someone else is always poised to step in and embarrass you with appeals to 'cultural purity'.* (34–35)

In his concerted efforts to de-mystify the techniques and content of didjeridu practices, McMahon has emphasised the experimental nature of his performances, in attempting to 'create sounds that have not been heard' in original traditional Aboriginal contexts.

McMahon can arguably be placed alongside Paul Kelly, Midnight Oil, Shane Howard and others whose incorporation of notions of Aboriginality 'isn't necessarily genetic; rather, it seems to be inflected epistemologically' (Lawe Davies, 1993: 58). However, the Aboriginal aspects tend to be confined to the politicised content of songs (ranging from Kelly's *Special Treatment* to Midnight Oils' *Beds Are Burning*). While much of McMahon's material attempts to represent the evocative aural soundscapes of the Western Desert region and other remote areas (the 'site as text' approach mentioned earlier), McMahon's work cannot be said to be overtly political in the same manner as Kelly and others (although he has consistently supported musical projects involved in Aboriginal causes, such as the 1988 'Building Bridges' project organised by the National Coalition of Aboriginal Organisations).

In examining the various definitions and uses of postmodern textuality, Collins (1989) puts forward the notion of 'juxtaposition as interrogation' which he defines as 'a careful, purposeful consideration of representational alternatives – rather than by simple pastiche or the "plundering" of history of art as though it were an attic filled with the artefacts of one's ancestor' (140). He goes on to argue that 'discursive juxtapositions do not result in the "emptying out" of all styles [but] form the basis of a productive engagement with antecedent and contemporary modes of organising experience' (ibid).

In this chapter I have taken up Collins' notion and argued that the politicisation of McMahon's work lies not in its style or content, but in the simple, yet loaded interpretations which stem from a non-Aboriginal Australian performing the didjeridu to such an involved extent. The juxtaposition of 'white man/black instrument' opens up a discursive space within the loaded semiotics of 'authenticity' which surround uses of the instrument. In Collins' terms, McMahon has provided a 'representational alternative' for the didjeridu which avoids plundering its ritualistic forms. He also avoids the subsequent reification of the didjeridu's other cultural properties and the more dubious claims made in association with world music.

Acknowledgements: Thanks to Charlie McMahon for his time; Karl Neuenfeldt, Philip Hayward and Justine Lloyd for comments on earlier drafts; and Kymberlie Harrison at Oceanic Music.

Notes

1. See Yunupingu, 1992: 34 for further discussion.

2. See Hayward, P. 'Safe, Exotic and Somewhere Else'; Lawe Davies, C 'Black Rock in Broome'; and Nicol, L 'Custom, Culture and Collaboration' - all in *Perfect Beat* v1 n2, January 1993.

3. I use Bob Hodge's (1990) term 'Aboriginalism' to discuss the ways in which Aborigines are constructed in a binary fashion of 'primitive' or 'civilised'.

4. McMahon has inspired a tribute band of sorts, with a Los Angeles group, Terra Incognita, 'styling themselves after our first record, but I can hardly imagine anyone doing a cover of our stuff; each style is so personal'.

5. McMahon in the video *Didjeridu With Charlie McMahon* (1992).

6. McMahon explored new anthropological territory in 1984 'discovering' nine nomadic Pintubi who had no previous contact with the non-Aboriginal population.

7. For example, Alan Dargin and Michael Atherton's 1991 *Bloodwood: The Art of the Didjeridu* recording which fuses didjeridu with Dobro guitars, synthesisers, drums and double bass.

8. Plastic sliding didjeridus ('slidjeridus') have now also become popular in England.

9. See Neuenfeldt, 1994: 99–100 on the outrageous claims of the associated properties and

benefits of the didjeridu made in an advertisement in the United States in 1991, which contains all the sincerity of a snake oil advertisement.

10. McMahon has stated that 'there are some things that no matter how long you stay in the bush, you're never going to get if you haven't been brought up with certain Aboriginal traditions' (*Didjeridu with Charlie McMahon* video).

11. See No Fixed Address' 1981 film *Wrong Side of the Road* for an insight into active discrimination against Aboriginal bands on the live pub circuit.

12. McMahon was hit by a beer-can playing in Canberra with the band Mixed Relations in front of a predominantly Koori audience. The person responsible later apologised. This is the only instance McMahon can recall of Aboriginal audiences questioning his performances.

Bibliography

Castles J. (1992) 'Tjungariganyi: Aboriginal Rock' in Hayward, P (ed) *From Pop To Punk To Postmodernism*, Sydney: Allen and Unwin.

Collins J. (1989) *Uncommon Cultures: Popular Culture and Postmodernism*, New York: Routledge.

Lawe Davies C. (1989) 'Looking for Signs of Style in Contemporary Popular Aboriginal Music', *Australian Journal of Communication* n16.

Lawe Davies C. (1993) 'Black Rock and Broome: Musical and Cultural Specificities', *Perfect Beat* v1 n2, January.

Hodge R. (1990) 'Aboriginal Truth and White Media: Eric Michaels Meets the Spirit of Aboriginalism', *Continuum* v3 n2.

Magowan F. (1996) 'Out of Time, Out of Place' (this volume)

Mitchell T. (1996) *Real Wild Child: Australian Popular Music and National Identity*, Oxford: Cassells.

Moyle A. (1981) 'The Australian Didjeridu: A Late Musical Intrusion', *World Archaeology* v12 n3.

Muecke S. (1992) *Textual Spaces: Aboriginality and Cultural Studies*, Sydney: New South Wales University Press.

Murphie A. (1996) 'Sound At The End Of The World As We Know It', *Perfect Beat* v2 n4, January.

Neuenfeldt K. (1993) 'The Didjeridu and the Overdub', *Perfect Beat* v1 n2, January

Neuenfeldt K. (1994) 'The Essentialistic, the Exotic, the Equivocal and the Absurd: The Cultural Production and Use of the Didjeridu in World Music' *Perfect Beat* v2 n1, July.

O'Donnell J. (1991) 'Midnight Oil' *Rolling Stone* [Australia] n459 July

Taussig M. (1993) *Mimesis and Alterity: A Particular History of the Senses* New York: Routledge.

Williams R. (1994) 'Sounds of Mother Earth' *The Australian Way* [Qantas Airline In-flight Magazine].

Yunupingu M. (1992) 'Black and White' *Rolling Stone* [Australia] n471, June.

Discography

Gondwanaland *Terra Incognita*, Hot Records, 1984

Gondwanaland *Let The Dog Out*, Hot Records, 1986

Gondwanaland *Gondwanaland*, WEA, 1987

Gondwanaland *Wildlife*, WEA, 1989

Gondwanaland *Wide Skies*, Warner, 1992

Gondwana *Travelling Songs*, Log Music, 1994

Charlie McMahon *Tjilatjila*, Logc Music, 1996

Midnight Oil *Red Sails In The Sunset*, CBS/Sony, 1985

Videography

Koori: A Will To Win (1987) CS Productions

Didjeridu With Charlie McMahon (1992) Gaia Films

Until The End Of The World (1991) Village Roadshow

Black Fella White Fella (1987) ABC/Sony

Chapter Nine

THE DIDJERIDU AND ALTERNATIVE LIFESTYLERS' RECONSTRUCTION OF SOCIAL REALITY

PATRICIA SHERWOOD

Alternative lifestylers in Australian society have been variously described as the 'counterculture', 'hippies' or 'dropouts' in the 1960s and 1970s; and as rural re-settlers, or 'greenies' in the 1980s and 1990s. Essentially, 'alternative lifestyler' is a conglomerate descriptive term covering a wide variety of life-styles, urban and rural, individual and communal, employed and unemployed, middle and working class, religious and secular. It is a term used to denote those who share a common concern with reconstructing society so as to create a cultural and social milieu that is based on co-operative, sustainable 'quality' personal, social and ecological relationships. In reconstructing reality, they appropriate cultural artefacts and beliefs from third or fourth world cultures. As an anthro-pologist involved in alternative lifestyle communities over the past twenty years, I have examined how many artefacts and beliefs from traditional cultures have been used by alternative lifestylers to build their model societies. In this chapter, I focus upon their use of one artefact, the didjeridu. It is more powerful than many other artefacts that they borrow such as yurts, tepees and sweat-lodges because of its connection with Aboriginal Australia, to which Australian alternative lifestylers look for inspiration of how to create holistic social forms. Other

139

instruments used by some alternative lifestylers include flutes and drums, but didjeridu is favoured and its use is more widespread because of its purported ideological compatibility with their urgent need to reconnect with the Australian land. (Note: all quotations from alternative lifestylers are, unless otherwise specified, taken from interviews with the author conducted in 1994 and are indicated by the abbreviation i/v.)

The alternative lifestylers' model society is based on four essential elements; firstly, holism of experience; secondly, community with its qualities of interrelatedness and co-operation; thirdly, ecology with its sustainable ethos; and fourthly, a creative spiritual milieu. Underlying these elements is the recognition that human beings comprise feelings, minds, souls and bodies and that their well-being depends on developing cultural forms that nourish all these aspects as well as creating healthy interrelationships with other human beings and the natural environment. In order to create this new reality, alternative lifestylers reject mainstream industrial society with its materialistic ethos, specialisation, profit motive, competition, fragmentation and alienation. They vigorously attack the monetary system of the corporate state. As Cock (1979) argued, when reviewing alternative lifestylers in Australia:

> To alternative Seekers, money was the symbol of the meaninglessness of the Corporate State and its false sense of wealth and security ... They attempted where possible to exchange items rather than buy. (222)

Metcalf (cited in Schwartz, 1990: 1) estimates that as many as 90,000 Australians may be full and proper participants in the alternative lifestyle movement, which is growing by about 10 per cent per year. He describes their values as incorporating a rejection of materialism, a yearning for a spiritual element lacking in mainstream religion and a concern for the environment. It is their rejection of materialism that differentiates them from the New Age movement which has become, in many cases, a highly commercialised and profit making industry. In contrast, alternative lifestylers look to the low consumption, low cost lifestyles of third and fourth world cultures to provide them with cultural motifs, traditions, roles and practices which they see as harmonious with their values. The demographic profile of alternative lifestylers has moved from a concentration of people in their teens and twenties during the 1970s, to a concentration of people in their thirties and forties in the 1990s (Schwartz: 1). They engage in the process of consciously constructing and reconstructing social and cultural reality. Berger and Luckmann in their classic work *The Construction of Social Reality* elucidate the process of reconstructing social reality, concluding that 'society ... [is] made by men, inhabited by men and, in turn, making men, in an ongoing historical process' (211). This process (excluding the sexist language), is clearly applicable to an analysis of the alternative lifestyle scene, particularly given their self-proclaimed constructionist position.

Traditional Aboriginal society provides a wealth of motifs for the alternative lifestylers. A special celebration issue of the *Nimbin News* (September 1983) commemorated the first gathering of alternative lifestylers there in 1974. The cover had a drawing of an Aboriginal Lizard man, whose outstretched arms encompassed a rainbow and which included the following words:

> *Behold the beauty of the re emergence of the sun, the dreaming law. Behold the wheel turns once more in the place of the beginnings. The clans grow like plants in the morning sun. The totems renewed, the dreaming again. Behold the wheel turns once more in the place of its beginnings ... The earth and I are one ... the land is my soul.*
> (cited in Newton, 1988: 53)

Australian alternative lifestylers' use of Aboriginal motifs and cultural elements in the construction of their reality will be illustrated by examining their use of didjeridu in the construction of social forms as they strive to build model societies based on their four essential elements of holism of experience; community, with its qualities of interrelatedness and co-operation; ecology, with its sustainable ethos; and a creative-spiritual milieu.

The didjeridu and the reconstruction of society based on holism

The scene is Nanga, a deserted mill town, on the banks of the Murray river, 80 kilometres south-east of Perth, Western Australia. The 'Nangariginals', as this group of alternative lifestylers call themselves, have gathered here together to celebrate the Australia Day weekend in alternative style. They seek new holistic meanings and cultural experiences. Central to the activities of the 'Nangariginals' is the didjeridu. As one of the 'Nangariginals' records in his Nanga diary:

> *Didgeridoo booms out in the voice of an ancient culture. The spirit of this land is running in our blood ... A few drummers come to put rhythm into the tribe. Dance away the contradiction and pain of city living.*
> (Selleck, 1979a: 13)

As this account testifies, didjeridu was an integral part of the symbolic and musical tradition of the alternative lifestylers in the 1970s, well before it was popularised in contemporary popular music and became a profitable, saleable commodity in the tourist and world music scene. It was, for alternative lifestylers in Australia, a metaphor of holism which was seen as uniting them with the earth, with each other, with sustainable lifestyles and with all living things. The didjeridu has provided alternative lifestylers who have played or experienced its sounds, with the feelings that it can be used to create a sense of unity with the past and the present, the natural and the human, the body and the soul. As Sky, an alternative lifestyler explained:

*Alternative lifestyler collecting hallucinogenic fungi ('magic mushrooms') while carrying a
didjeridu (still from* Fungimentary, *1995). [Photo: courtesy of Paul G. Blake, Peckinpah Films.]*

> *Didjeridu roots me down into the earth ... all of the earth. I feel incredibly
> cleansed and centred, very whole when I play didj ... It connects one
> deeply back into the earth, into the rhythms of the land, of the creatures,
> of the trees, of all living things.* (i/v)

These sentiments are clearly expressed by Ron Nagorska citing the words of
Wanjuk Marika when explaining how the didjeridu has changed his life:

> *I am of the earth. I am a son of the earth. I am the trees, the rivers, the
> rocks. I am kin to earth's creatures. I am kin to earth's creation. The
> earth is my mother.* (i/v)

Angie, a white, female didjeridu player from the traditional Aboriginal country
in the Kimberleys, in the north of Western Australia, reports that didjeridu has
the powerful capacity to create feelings of wholeness, to get one in touch with
the essential and primal links of experience. She explains:

> *When I play didjeridu the instrument just gives me the opportunity to
> open to all life ... then I can create this experience for others by playing
> the didjeridu to them.* (i/v)

This view is repeatedly shared by many alternative lifestyle didjeridu players who consciously represent the didjeridu as creating these holistic experiences and as 'tuning them in' to Aboriginality which they perceive in terms of a primal connectedness to the earth. While some alternative lifestylers create this representation out of their contact with traditional Aboriginal people, other alternative lifestylers are simply basing their perception on the 'noble savage' image. This mythologising is a type of stereotyping and falls into Langton's second category of cultural construction of Aboriginality (1994) which she acutely defines as occurring within Anglo Australians and not in dialogue with Aborigines. (100)

The didjeridu and the reconstruction of community

Alternative lifestylers have a passion to create a sense of community and 'belongingness' to a meaningful whole. Cock (1979) reveals in his survey of alternative lifestylers that 97 per cent of his respondents had a clear commitment to decentralisation which meant the 'establishment' of self-governing semi-autonomous communities. (227) The alternative lifestylers' sense of community is akin to Turner's (1969) description of 'communitas' which he contrasts with 'societas'. Communitas is characterised by egalitarianism, communalism, co-operation, sharing, a spiritual ethos, simplicity, homogeneity and totality and is contrast to 'societas' which is characterised by dehumanising social structures, hierarchies, competition, materialism, complexity, heterogeneity and fragmentation. (129) Thus, for alternative lifestylers, traditional societies, particularly Aboriginal communities in Australia, are represented as providing a rich tapestry of living communal experiences to which they can turn for their source of inspiration as they attempt to recreate community.

One of the major preoccupations of alternative lifestylers has been to reconstruct social gatherings that foster a sense of interconnectedness and interrelatedness amongst participants. Confests and Down to Earth Festivals provide large public forums for their attempts to recreate meaningful communal and community experiences. Alternative lifestylers from different communities or who live as couples, or singles, gather at such forums to celebrate the healthy lifestyle they believe they are creating. These are the powerful events which foster large scale affirmation of the new lifestyle. Cock and Lavery (1975) reflecting on the experiences of the Moora Moora community members near Healesville in Victoria, capture this social fragmentation that alternative lifestylers are trying to repair:

> [We] *are particularly concerned about the isolation and loneliness of suburban living ... We regret the superficiality of our human relationships within the suburban street ... the alienation between learning and living ... Many of us are discontented with the mainstream of our society, the direction in which we are going. We dislike the over centralised*

143

*nature of our society, our non-participation in the decisions that most
personally affect us. We resent being manipulated to 'Keep up with the
Joneses' and the competitive, violent and materialistic values that per-
meate the wider society.* (54)

In their quest for community, they attempt to reconstruct the tribal ethic complete
with campfire and didjeridu, as Selleck (1979b) recounts when he describes the
activities of the Nangariginals. Their tribal reassertion is symbolised by the circle
around the campfire which becomes a pivotal site for recreating a sense of
togetherness. The didjeridu is used to recreate their feelings of unity with each
other and the land. Story telling and music making are seen as ways of providing
for a healthy individual and community spirit in a natural setting:

> *The accent of the festival was nature as a way of life ... Every human has
> a naturally balanced character that will blossom and grow if treated with
> tenderness and care. The true nature of humans is not aggressive but
> passive and inherently good. By becoming familiar with a naturally
> balanced forest the good feeling of human kind is released from the
> conditioned pain response and aggression of our unnatural society.*
> (Selleck 1979b: 40)

Cock (1979) argues that the re-emerging need for community reflects the extreme
developments of our culture which have led us to hold the false consciousness
that we can live separately from other human beings and from the planet earth.
Alternative lifestylers recognise this alienation and are committed to producing
cultural forms that reconnect people together. Ingamells and Foote (1986),
writing on the Agni Farm community at Kin Kin in Queensland, address the
crucial issues of reconstructing community, proposing a triangular process of
empowered individuals creating social structures which 'connect people in
vibrant and meaningful patterns' (142).

The didjeridu is one instrument that is being used as a pivotal force for producing
renewed social structures that support community. This is illustrated by Sky
recounting how she sees didjeridu creating community among alternative lifestylers. Sky, an experienced didjeridu player, began by describing the didjeridu
as a 'channel', a channel of the energy of the surrounding environment and of
the people who have lived and shared in that environment:

> *Didjeridu enables one to tune in to the spirit of the place ... the spirit
> energy of the place which is determined by the energy of the natural
> environment and the human activities that have occurred there ... Some
> places have very strong energy like this place down south where I played
> near some water ... The didjeridu channelled the power of that place and
> when a group of people are listening to that sort of energy they become*

united, energised, captured by the spirit of the place which the didj announces. But in other places ... well the energy isn't really there ... it's flat, sort of empty ... and when you try to play didjeridu there it doesn't really capture people's attention ... They become inattentive and easily distracted ... A didjeridu player can't create energy if it's not in the place ... with very rare exceptions ... That's why I rarely play didjeridu in the city ... it's a land instrument. (i/v)

Traditional didjeridu playing was incorporated in a community tradition of song and storytelling and alternative lifestylers' attempts to recreate this tradition. Although they are rarely informed about the ancient spiritual songs and stories accompanying didjeridu, they create their own out of their experiences of urban alienation and yearning for a place in the natural world. Williams (63) tells how traditional skilled didjeridu players moved from tribe to tribe, a pattern characterising the didjeridu alternative players. High levels of mobility between communities of alternative lifestylers, especially the young, mean that the didjeridu players frequently spread their music making over a wide area. They travel to significant events whether births, deaths, forest gatherings or celebrations. In Western Australia two didjeridu players described to me their movements over several months in 1994 and they included distances over 3000 kilometres, from Broome in the North West, to Denmark in the South West of the state. Angie, a didjeridu player in the Kimberleys, commented that in that region alone there were dozens of non-Aboriginal didjeridu players, many who travelled around from one place to another, or who live itinerant lifestyles. The didjeridu has become a symbol of a particular type of seeker. Angie explained:

When you meet another didjeridu player you know that you're both going to end up playing didjeridu together. When I was travelling through India with my didj, I met lots of other white people travelling with their didjeridus. Didj has a way of linking you up with people, you know immediately that you are going to play didj together ... Didjeridu just binds you together ... it is not like flute or some other instruments ... they don't have this power to draw you together into a community. (i/v)

Of those alternative lifestylers who learn to play didjeridu, they do so because of their experiences of listening to didjeridu played by other alternative lifestylers. Some who learn didjeridu say that they were motivated by its power to make them feel whole; others emphasise the experience they derive from playing it which connects them with the earth; while others emphasise the experience of healing that they attribute to listening to the sound of the didjeridu. There are communities of friends who play didjeridu and didjeridu provides the fabric for the participants to weave a communal experience.

Essentially, then, the didjeridu experience is represented by alternative lifestylers

145

who play the instrument and/or who listen to it, as providing feelings of whole-ness and opportunities to create a shared reality with other people and communities.

The dideridu and the expression of an ecological and sustainable ethos

Alternative lifestylers use the didjeridu to create what they describe as a sense of re-connectedness with the earth, their mother, who has been raped and brutalised by industrial society. Again Selleck vividly describes this experience at Nanga:

> The forest looks on, unsure. A short distance away human-kind has forced its greed upon the perfect balance of nature. Open cut mines lie as a cancer upon the body of the Earth. The trees watch in fear of what Man can do. Trust in people is slowly gained as they walk around picking up broken glass and rusty iron. Bad memories of human kind removed. Ground work done, stages are constructed, toilet dug, a mud brick sauna is built, showers, swings, play ground, kitchen, tents. The people smiling, happy, expectant. Slowly, familiar faces dissolve into a crowd of happy loving people. The children [have] a tribal feast in a shady grove while parents explored, always a conversation to tune in to, a smiling face, a hug of togetherhood. (1979a: 10)

At the 1979 Confest alternative lifestylers consulted the Aborigines they had invited and asked for help to create a new relationship with the land. Ken Colbung, an Aboriginal elder from Perth spoke to them, stating:

> We have to replace for Mankind what mankind has taken from Mother earth. Mother earth is a sick mother, we are like children on the breast of Mother earth: sucking but not milk. (cited in Selleck 1979a:10)

Through didjeridu, alternative lifestylers believe that they can hear the voice of the land and of the earth's living creatures, which reawakens within themselves their strong feelings for a sustainable ecological relationship with the earth. Forest, a young didjeridu player in the alternative scene, reflects this view when she attributes supernatural powers to the didjeridu: 'Didj chooses you and it will teach you'. (i/v) For alternative lifestylers, the didjeridu is sometimes considered to have real supernatural powers. Like crystals, mandalas and mantras, the didjeridu is sometimes described as emitting powerful vibrations and energies that profoundly direct and influence the behaviours of persons who come into contact with them. Didjeridu is then personified and ascribed by some alternative lifestylers as the teacher or connecter with mother earth. As Sky adds: 'Didj is primarily a land instrument not a performance instrument. It communicates the

146

soul of the land'. (i/v) Angie notes: 'didj provides you with a direct link with the earth ... with the natural environment ... in all its primal power'. (i/v)

The alternative lifestylers' sense of ecological sustainability is tied up with a rejection of the over reliance on the money economy (Trainer, 1988: 28). Alternative trading schemes such as LETS (Local Energy Transfer System) reflect this desire to recreate an economy based on the real worth of goods and services, not on artificial movements of money in the money markets. As a musical instrument, the didjeridu fits clearly into this new economy. As William, an alternative lifestyler who plays didjeridu, explained to me:

> *Didj is one of my favourite instruments. It's got everything going for it. You can make it yourself out of natural materials. You don't need a mine or smelter like you do with so any Western instruments ... It's an instrument that is really low cost ... natural and blends in with the natural environment.* (i/v)

William's sentiments were frequently reiterated by other alternative lifestylers, both players and listeners alike. They admire the accessibility of didjeridu to creation by crafts people without destruction of the natural environment. It epitomises their idea of an environmentally friendly and sustainable product.

The didjeridu and the experience of the spiritual/creative dimension

Frequently, alternative lifestylers will comment on the didjeridu's capacity to reawaken their spiritual and/or creative selves. Duncan described it as: 'a spiritual experience that reawakens your links with your spirit and the spirit of the earth'. (i/v) Sky expressed another common sentiment about the spiritual power of didjeridu for the alternative lifestyler; namely, its power to assist individualistic Westernised persons to 'let go of ego' and to experience the 'soul of the land'. Alternative lifestylers are attempting to construct a spirituality that links themselves and the natural environment and to represent traditional indigenous peoples, particularly Australian Aborigines, as holding the key to this spirituality that arises from the natural environment. As Forest explained to me: 'the didjeridu enables us to be led back into our spiritual selves, our connectedness with Mother Earth that we have lost in industrial society'. (i/v) These patterns of spiritual experiences that alternative lifestylers associate with the playing of the didjeridu have been succinctly identified by Neuenfeldt (1994) where he describes essentialistic uses of the didjeridu as twofold:

> *One is an essentialistic spirituality which is sometimes conflated with notions of indigenous people as stewards of the natural environment still in touch with its essence where the didjeridu becomes a resonator, if you*

147

will, of Mother Earth; the other is a perception of the didjeridu as a conduit between the sacred and the profane. (93)

Several alternative lifestylers emphasised the power of didjeridu to produce a meditative state in the player. Angie commented that for her and for many other women players, didjeridu is primarily an instrument that evokes spiritual experience, that connects one with one's centre, providing a meditative sound. In my ethnographic data, it was much more common for female players to represent the didjeridu as evoking spiritual experiences than it was with males, who more often represented it as having primal power to link people up with the land or themselves.

Waters in his foreword to his ethnography of Hopi mystical (1963) experiences speaks of the 'psychic chasm' separating Western rational materialism from 'red America, black Africa, yellow Asia and the brown Middle East' (i/v). He could well have added black Australia. Members of the alternative scene often construct a reality whereby the didjeridu is attributed with the power to evoke spiritual experiences. In this view, the didjeridu enables them to access the sacred dimension of life, not in terms of an external all-powerful deity, but in terms of an all-embracing energy or presence within the individual, the group and in all natural phenomena. For other alternative lifestylers, the didjeridu is attributed with the ability to enable them to access the non-material dimensions of experience, through assisting the listener and/or player to enter an altered state of consciousness. As Duncan, an alternative lifestyler, described it to me: 'it has a meditative quality ... just listening to it can take you away into another dimension of experience ... to a spiritual consciousness'. (i/v)

Guy Grant (a qualified medical practitioner), who uses didjeridu as an unconventional method of healing particularly in the areas of stuttering, confirms the alternative lifestylers' view that didjeridu can be used to produce altered states of consciousness through chanting and blowing as a player and can also produce meditative states in both players and listeners. He states that the shape of the didjeridu is akin to the shape of the human windpipe and it produces a vibration through the body that provides the venue for a spiritual force to come through the player. (i/v)

Several of the female alternative lifestyle didjeridu players who were interviewed commented on their use of didjeridu to produce healing vibrations for ill friends. The use of the didjeridu in a healing context was more common among female players than male players. One cited an especially powerful experience of five women didjeridu players joining together to provide healing energies for an ill friend. Workshops on didjeridu playing that attract alternative lifestylers often emphasise the spiritual and healing effects of didjeridu for players. This is exemplified by this excerpt from an advertisement:

Physically the process of Circular Breathing helps to clear the sinuses and lungs. Many who have suffered from problems in these areas, including Asthma, have reported marked improvement. Psychically, many have reported an easy transition to the meditative state simply by listening to the sound of the Didjeridu. The Didjeridu seems to have an ability to act upon all Chakras – though most Didjeridus are in the lower chakra keys (C, C#, D, E). Listeners and players of the Didjeridu report feelings of Communion with the Earth, contact with Spiritual Guides, Healing of body pains and release of tension – all higher Chakra qualities. (Davey, 1994: unpaginated)

Incorporated into such accounts of spiritual experiences with the didjeridu, are the concepts and world views of alternative lifestylers on spirituality. Chakras and meditation are all concepts borrowed and fused with the instrument of didjeridu to produce a new spiritual reality that reflects the eclectic cultural roots of the alternative lifestyle tradition. The facility with which reality is reconstructed and cultural experience reproduced give it the authentic flavour of ancient spiritual traditions. For example, the chakra key is a concept derived from a fusion of Hindu spiritual teachings on the chakra or energy centres of the human being and New Age theology on musical and colour correspondences to each of these chakras.

Appraisal of alternative lifestylers' use of didjeridu to construct their social reality

Didjeridu is used extensively to produce and reproduce alternative lifestylers' Eurocentric dreams of a better world based on the four key elements of holistic meaning, of co-operative community, sustainable lifestyle and spiritual vitality. Few alternative lifestylers that I have interviewed over the past 20 years, have shown an in-depth understanding of Aboriginal culture and of didjeridu. There is a strong sense of identifying Aboriginal culture as a utopian ideal and it is believed that elements drawn from it have the power to help Westerners reconstruct a sense of connectedness with the land, the earth and living things. Parkhill (1993) notes how this utopian view transforms traditional music practices: 'Complexes of social meaning originally associated with time honoured musical traditions are now endowed with a non specific, non directional depth by the cover note writers' Eurocentric dreams'. (503)

Not only is the didjeridu idealised as it is incorporated into alternative lifestylers' society, but it is also imbued with powers that transcend its human creators. It is consciously endowed with a will of its own, with the power to direct the wills and feelings of both players and listeners. This perception of the didjeridu powerfully confirms alternative lifestylers' desire to live in a world where their emotions and spirits can experience things not subject to rational, intellectual

149

scrutiny. In this constructed world, feelings and intuitions provide more valid experiences than rational thoughts alone.

The didjeridu is perceived by some alternative lifestylers as providing a bridge to facilitate the journey of white Australians back to the land, themselves and each other. They recognise that it is a different connectedness to that experienced by traditional Aboriginal peoples, but they see themselves making an effort to reconnect and are critical of other white Australians who continue to be seduced and fragmented by the hedonistic lifestyle of Western industrial society. In this sense, didjeridu has been incorporated into their reconstructed society as an instrument of expiation which absolves its new users of many of the sins of Western society.

The difficulties inherent in the process of recontextualising the didjeridu in the alternative lifestyle scene are illustrated by two incidents. The first illustrates issues that arise from gender role renegotiation. How do alternative lifestylers deal with the view that didjeridu is an instrument reserved for males? One recontextualisation of the issue is the implementation of a social rule constructed by many female didjeridu players in traditional Aboriginal communities. Angie explained to me that it was fine for a woman to play didjeridu if she was white, but not if she was Aboriginal. (i/v) However, a white woman should not play didjeridu before Aboriginal male elders who had been through the Law. The second incident illustrates the difficulties of developing new social rules and norms to govern the appropriate use of a traditional instrument. Burnam Burnam (1987) recounts a happening involving didjeridu at an alternative festival in the late 1970s:

> *One Down to Earth Festival followed the other – until I received a devastating shock at the Berri Festival in South Australia. An Aboriginal Arts, Craft and Musical Festival was being held simultaneously in nearby Adelaide. I journeyed from Berri and enticed a bus-load of traditional performers from the Olmbulgarri-Kununurra area of the Kimberley region of Western Australia. By arrangement they were to perform around a campfire hosted by white 'hippies'. The didjeridu players, clap stick artists, singers and dancers were performing when, to my horror, a nude male crazily picked up the end of the didjeridu while it was being played and placed his erect penis into it. The horror and shame of that single act made me hate whites. I was to miss the next five annual Down to Earth Festivals because of the sickness and irreverence of that one act. My feelings of revulsion were all the more intense as I knew that the performers came from an area which had seen the destruc-tion of their burial sites and hunting grounds by white men. (97)*

Alternative lifestylers run the risk, in the process of reconstructing and reproducing another cultural form, of producing a new reality that is offensive to the traditional culture or of failing to have sufficient new rules developed to protect the use of objects that they have incorporated into their new society.

Conclusion

There are four positive outcomes for alternative lifestylers' use of didjeridu in the construction of alternative societies. These include: firstly, the experience of personal healing; secondly, the experience of re-connectedness with the earth which provides a greening of their consciousness and which potentiates their commitment to sustainable environmental practices; thirdly, an experience of the spiritual/creative to counter the void and alienation in their over-industrialised and technologised lives; and fourthly, bridging experiences which help connect them in positive ways to Aboriginal peoples and their cultures.

Firstly, many alternative lifestylers talked about the healing potential of didjeridu which they had experienced either as players or as listeners. In particular, Guy Grant spoke about its healing power for stuttering, while others mentioned a variety of disorders including asthma and stress. Didjeridu was most frequently named by alternative lifestylers for its relaxing healing powers and female didjeridu players, more often than males, recounted using the didjeridu to facilitate healing in ill friends.

Secondly, all alternative lifestylers interviewed about didjeridu mentioned its power to reconnect them with the natural environment, a quality that they saw greatly needed in industrialised society, which in their view, has lost touch with the earth. This is reflected in such comments featured in the *Nimbin News*, the alternative lifestyle mouthpiece for the Nimbin area:

> *The land is my soul, your soul. We must not be separated from our soul*
> *if man is to survive this earthly sojourn, we must attune ourselves to*
> *planetary spiritualism.* (cited in Newton, 1988: 67)

Clearly, alternative lifestylers tend to support a sustainable approach to the earth, a positive asset in mainstream society beset by the problems of unsustainable environmental values. Alternative lifestylers are able to re-introduce this needed value base of sustainability into mainstream society. It is frequently these persons who are in environmental protest movements. A recent forest blockade against logging of old growth forests in Western Australia had, as its dominant numerical representation, alternative lifestylers. Several of these activists play didjeridu and attribute much of their wakened feelings towards the earth to their spiritual experiences derived from their playing.

Thirdly, the didjeridu has provided a medium for spiritual experiences for a number of alternative lifestylers, as detailed above in the section on spirituality.

This re-created type of spirituality using the didjeridu gives participants the positive experiences of a sense of purpose and direction, an experience of the transcendent and a sense of place in the world. Belief systems give the believers a sense of power and purpose in their personal and social lives and didjeridu playing is enabling some alternative lifestylers to construct a meaningful belief system for themselves.

Fourthly, the playing of didjeridu by alternative lifestylers who incorporate it in their efforts to construct a new tribal ethos has led to a reaching out to understand Aboriginal peoples and culture in a new way that other white Australians have ignored. Certainly, some of this reaching out by alternative lifestylers has resulted in an idealisation of the Aboriginal way of life, but it has also sensitised alternative lifestylers to social justice issues that affect Aborigines in Australia, particularly in terms of land rights, sacred sites and mining issues (Newton, 1988: 67). Alternative lifestylers are highly represented among movements and protests supporting Aboriginal social justice issues. It is as though they have recognised the value of Aboriginal respect for the land.

In essence, alternative lifestyles in Australia have used didjeridu as one element, albeit a powerful element, in their quest to construct a culture that is based on the four central patterns of providing holistic experiences for the individual, of creating a tribal ethos where experiences of community are prized, of providing a sustainable integrated environmental consciousness and of creating a spirituality where all living things are linked to each other and the earth. Although in the construction of this new culture, the traditional Aboriginal culture may be idealised and its values transformed or distorted from a traditional perspective, for the alternative lifestyler this new social reality is meaningful and powerful in transforming their lives. It is cultural elements such as the didjeridu that act as a conduit of power from the past, to revitalise the present reality and to rekindle hope in a future.

Bibliography

Berger P. and Luckmann T. (1979) *The Social Construction of Reality*, Auckland: Peregrine.

Black P. (1983) 'Australian Communes: Retreat to the Third and Fourth Worlds', (unpublished) ANZAAS Conference (Perth) paper.

Burnam Burnam, (1987) 'Aboriginal Australia and the Green Movement', in Hutton, D. (ed).

Cock P. (1979) *Alternative Australia*, Melbourne: Quartet.

Cock P. (1993) 'Redeveloping Intentional Communities for the 21st Century', *Community Quarterly*, n29.

Cock P. and Lavery B. (1975) 'Moora Moora', *Earth Garden* n12.

Davey R. (1994) Promotional Pamphlet for 'Didjeridoo Workshops and Schnupperabend' – self-published (c/o Lot 11 Traylen Road Stoneville, Western Australia 6081).

Hutton D. (ed) (1979) *Green Politics in Australia*, Ryde (NSW): Angus and Robertson.

Ingamels A. and Foote R. (1986) 'A Community of Intention: Agni Farm Co-operative, Kin Kin, Queensland.' *People Working Together* v2.

Langton M. (1994) 'Aboriginal Art and Film: the Politics of Representation', *Race and Class* v35 n4.

Leggett D. (1987) 'Building Communities: the Green Alternative', in Hutton, D. (ed).

Nagorcka R. (1981) 'How the Didjeridu has Changed my Life', (unpublished) International Music and Technology Conference (Melbourne) paper.

Neuenfeldt K. (1994) 'The Essentialistic, the Exotic, The Equivocal and the Absurd' *Perfect Beat* v2 n1, July.

Newton J. (1988) 'Aborigines, Tribes and the Counterculture' *Social Analysis* n23.

Parkhill P. (1993) 'Of Tradition, Tourism and the World Music Industry', *Meanjin* v2 n3.

Schwartz L. (1990) 'Hippies of the 90s', *The Age*, 18/2.

Selleck V. (1979a) 'Confest Report', *Down to Earth Magazine* v1 n45.

Selleck V. (1979b) 'Tree Festival Report', *Down to Earth Magazine* v1 n45.

Skandies J. (1991) 'Local Energy Created Out of Unemployment', *Social Alternatives* v10 n3.

Trainer T. (1988) 'Our Global Predicament', *National Outlook* v10 n8.

Turner V. (1969) *The Ritual Process*, London: Routledge and Kegan Paul.

Waters F . (1969) *Book of the Hopi*, New York: Ballantine.

Williams R. (1994) 'Sounds of Mother Earth' *The Australian Way* (Qantas magazine), May.

Thread Two

NOTIONS OF AUTHENTICITY:

A Discussion on Didjeridu Construction Materials

KARL NEUENFELDT (ed)

D iscussions that deal directly or indirectly with issues of 'authenticity' and didjeridu playing are common on the Dreamtime mailing list (didjeridu@eartha.mills.edu). Authenticity is notoriously hard to define but participants usually have strongly-held, if somewhat inconsistent, notions of what it is. One recurrent topic concerns the relative merits of different construction materials. Participants' opinions range from those who believe that didjeridus should be made with 'natural' and low-tech materials to those who believe they should be made with what ever is affordable, available and aesthetically pleasing, (even if 'un-natural' and hi-tech). Outside of Australia and also increasingly *in* Australia (due to the rapid depletion of certain valued woods) didjeridu makers are being forced to improvise. As a result both aspirant and established didjeridu players are turning to materials such as PVC and ABS plumbing pipe, resins, plastic golf-club liner tubes, bamboo, agave cactus, commercial woods, glass, fluorescent light tubes, rams horns and brass to manufacture didjeridus. Discussions concerning the 'authenticity' of materials reveal much about how authenticity is conceptualised, as well as how the didjeridu is evolving technologically. In the following discussion participants give conflicting advice and evaluations with a minimum of animosity. This thread, which developed in late 1995, presents participants' opinions on two common construction materials, plastic and wood.

... I noticed with concern the fact that a number of people use ABS [plastic] *to make didjeridus. I have done a lot of experimentation and research on didj making and have learned that ABS is a very toxic plastic. It should never be used in any circumstance that allows close contact, specifically breathing! It outgasses toxic petro-chemical fumes and the process is concentrated by any heat, including direct sunlight. In plumbing, ABS is only used for waste lines due to its toxicity, especially when heated ... I strongly urge people using ABS to at least consider the risks before playing them again. The Didjeridu is a beautiful and powerful instrument and playing didj has a number of health benefits. I will gladly do further research to determine the specific health risks if people are sceptical or concerned ...* (Alan Prichard)

... Long term health is too important to risk. I have learned how to make didjs out of fallen tree branches and Yucca stalks. These are far better sounding and looking than anything plastic and can be fabricated without any petrochemical materials (non-toxic wood glue and either home made egg tempera and non-petrochemical paints are what I use). The extra effort far outweighs the potential health risks. I am more than willing to share my knowledge of using natural materials if people are interested. (Tom Bray)

Regarding ABS and toxicity, you probably are suffering more from mercury poisoning from your [tooth] *fillings ... If you would like in-depth info on ABS constructions, I have built about 100 different versions: some I'll share, some not. Contact me directly or better yet come and visit. I have part of my didj course called 'fun with plastic'. Have fun.* (Randy Raine Reusch)

[Reply to Alan Prichard] *I laud your practice of making didjeridu's from natural materials. It sounds like you have made some wonderful instruments. I make didjeridus from ABS and was quite alarmed to read your report. I certainly do not want to be promulgating an idea that is going to cause harm to others. So I spent the entire day researching ABS ... I called three manufacturers and asked them if ABS pipe, when exposed to ambient or normal conditions with sunlight, produced toxic gases, they all said no ... Alan, ABS didjeridus can be made to look and sound wonderful. Happy didjing.* (Tom Bray)

Hey guys, I really think the plastic didj's are good to learn on, but they lack the character, both visual and auditory, of wooden instruments. Someone who visited me today summed it up when she said 'sounds' like' a didjeridu'. So, it is with this in mind that I ask if anyone knows where

The 'Didjeri-dudes' (left–right,Jamie Cunningham and Brian Pertl) performing on PVC didjeridus in Seattle (1995).

I can get natural materials, bamboo, someone mentioned yucca, etc. I haven't any termites lying about, so a pre-hollowed type of wood would make me ecstatic. Thanks for any help.
(Adam Adan)

... I can contribute the paltry knowledge that I have. Firstly, I have to point out that I have never played an ABS didj, but I have played PVC, cardboard poster tube, wood with a near perfect cylindrical bore, as well as a termite bored eucalyptus ozzie [Australian] *didj, oh and also bamboo originals. My feeling is that wood really does make a difference.* (Sean Borman)

Hi All. On a purely acoustic level there is nothing about a 'real' didj that is inherently better than a well formed plastic model. It's the interior shape that counts. As I have stated many times in the Didj Digest, my PVC and Bondo didjs made by Jim Wegner are as good or better than the best 'real' didjs I have every played and this includes the didjs that Yothu Yindi perform on. Even straight PVC, although it has a rather 'tubular sound' has a certain appeal ... most of the 'real' instruments that make it to the US are of pretty bad quality (unless you're willing to part with $400–600). (Brian Pertl)

... I would say that ABS and PVC are virtually the same in sound quality ... [Wooden Australian didjeridus] vary tremendously in playability and many instruments that people buy when touring Oz [Australia] are terrible because they don't have any idea how to select one for playability. The craftsmen know this and (I think) frequently sell nicely painted but hard-to-play instruments to tourists as art pieces ... For me there is no question that the best, sweetest, most interesting, etc. sounds come from termite bored wood and I believe that the variations and grooving made by the termites are significant in creating those sounds. (Geoff Brown)

... who can knock the 97 cent price [of a plastic didj made from a golf club tube]*! I have played several' real' d'dus & for all practical purposes (really) can just barely tell the difference between some of the plastic ones & a real one! The point is here one need not be totally devoted or immersed in a line of thinking to have one whale of a lot of fun none-the-less!* (Dennis Havlena)

I've seen this thread several times now and I have to make a comment. I have an Australian didgeridoo and by virtue of the shape of the branch and the way it was hollowed out, the tube is distinctly irregular. It is big at one end and smaller at the other and is not even close to circular in cross-section. This is much different from a mailing tube or a golf club tube and is bound to have a huge impact on the sound. A cylindrical tube is capable of producing only a limited set of harmonics, whereas an irregular tube will have a richer and more complex sound – usually described as more aesthetic to the ear. Add to this the resonance of the wood and you have a much different instrument than some of the plastic tube things I have seen people sell as didgeridoos. (Scott Shaw)

... I've played my PVC didj for several people, non-versed in the depths of didjeridu music and have found that folks consistently recognise the sound, even though what they've heard before is probably 'authentic' and what I'm playing is plastic. PVC has two things going for it that I think make it superior to an authentic didj for me at the moment: (1) it's easily worked (I play in a regular band and tuning the things are simply a matter of slicing off lengths of pipe until it's in tune) and (2) it's cheap! Not that this is likely to happen, but should I ever lose interest in playing 'em, I'm not out a huge sum of $$$. I've got a number of variations on the straight pipe theme and all in all, my whole set is still probably under $30. For five times that amount I might be able to get my hands on an 'authentic' didj, but there's no guarantee it'd be in any kind of tune to be played with other instruments. Actually there's three things going for

PVC: (3) it's the only kind of didj I've been able to get my hands on ...
Happy didjing! (Matthew Newby)

At a surface level, there are several points of interest in this Internet thread. One is that extra-musical concerns are sometimes paramount, concerns that have more to do with world view and lifestyle than aesthetics. Another is that availability is often the determining factor in choosing or championing a particular construction material. A third is that the technological knowledge of the proponents of plastic seems to be greater given that many have hands-on experience making their own instruments. At a deeper level, there are several further points of interest. One is that judgements of what is more or less 'authentic' are essentially aesthetic and difficult to quantify or justify. The actual sound produced by a wood or plastic didjeridu can be measured electronically but to what end ? The information would be of limited use given that natural and synthetic construction materials themselves vary considerably. Added to this, every player has different ways of playing and levels of ability. An untalented didjeriduist remains so regardless of their didjeridu's construction material (although novices might find didjeridus made of one or other material easier to learn on). Another point of interest is that there is recognition by some participants that in the Australian context the didjeridu industry is part of the mass tourism industry. A didjeridu is not necessarily better because it is made by an Aboriginal artisan. Quality varies widely. An 'authentic' wood didjeridu can be unplayable because it was made as an art piece and not a musical instrument.

Chapter Ten

OUT OF TIME, OUT OF PLACE

A Comparison of Applications of the Didjeridu in Aboriginal Australia, Great Britain and Ireland

FIONA MAGOWAN

In London's Covent Garden a relatively new musical sound filters through the cafes and along the cobbled streets. It is the deep rhythmic throb of the didjeridu. This ancient instrument of Aboriginal Australia is steadily gaining popularity amongst musicians and audiences in Britain and Ireland. Interest in the didjeridu has escalated since the 1980s with the rise of recording artists such as Cyrung, Shaun Farrenden, Stephen Kent, Shozo, Ianto Thornber, Graham Wiggins and the Irish/Australian group Reconciliation (comprising Phillip Conyngham, Maria Cullen, Alan Dargin and Simon O'Dwyer). Indeed, scattered across Britain and Ireland are a number of commercial outlets for the manufacture and sale of the didjeridu, as well as recordings featuring British and Irish didjeridu performers. But, why should this indigenous instrument of Aboriginal Australia hold such fascination in urban locales and constitute a part of so many alternative music festivals? What connection does it have with Irish music? What values and significance does its long conical shape and low droning sound convey to Westerners who play it? How much is really known about its traditional spiritual and ritual importance?[1]

In this chapter I will examine the extent to which the traditional role of the didjeridu in Aboriginal Australia has been appropriated by performers in Great Britain and Ireland to other genres and contexts, creating a synthesis of style, form and sound. In ethnomusicological research, what constitutes tradition, hybridity or synthesis have been considered as an alteration between an authentication of indigenous music or a *werktreue* ideal (the ideal of fidelity) and the problematics of such an ideal (Goehr, 1992: 243). This pendulum movement from musical authenticity to an ethnocentric appropriation of didjeridu style and context is a major concern of non-Aboriginal musicians. To explore both Western and Aboriginal musicians' perceptions of the nature of didjeridu soundscapes, I will profile some of the prominent producers of commercial didjeridu music and compare their work with indigenous ritual performance in Australia

In an age of a growing number of religious ideologies across Britain and Ireland, I will further attempt to account for perceived psychological, physiological and spiritual affects produced from the sounds and rhythms of the didjeridu. Incentives and ideologies will be examined through various performance styles leading to a consideration of the didjeridu as a vehicle of global unity in world musics. (Note: All comments attributed to British didjeridu players in this chapter are, unless otherwise specified, taken from interviews with the author conducted in 1995 and are indicated by the abbreviation 'i/v'.)

The rise of the didjeridu in Great Britain

Didjeridus first appeared around the turn of the century in Great Britain. They were collected for museums such as the Pitt Rivers Museum, Oxford, which obtained its first instrument from a Mr. Wilkins in 1900. It was brought back to Britain by J.V. Parkes from Port Essington in the Northern Territory in 1891.[2] Despite being a musical exhibit of intriguing form and design, no efforts were made to facilitate performance contexts in which the instrument could be played. Some museums now take this aspect of education into consideration in their exhibits. For example, in 1986 a diverse and comprehensive music collection was set up in the Balfour Building, Oxford. Today, all manner of musical instruments are on display but they are not just visually intriguing. Viewers can hear a variety of music, including Aboriginal didjeridu techniques and rhythms through headsets as they observe the instruments in a glass case.

Rolf Harris, one of Australia's best known entertainers, was the first person to introduce the British public to the music of the didjeridu. Starting his career in 1959 with *Tie Me Kangaroo Down Sport*, followed by singles such as *Sun Arise* (1962) and *Two Little Boys* (1969), Harris' humorous routines accompanied by washboard, wobbleboard and solo didjeridu items were to expose a curious public to the sounds of the instrument. Harris had learned to play didjeridu from David Blannasi, a well-regarded Aboriginal musician and painter from the Northern Territory. In his early twenties Harris moved to England to go to art school, supporting himself by performing in cabaret. Pursuing music, singing and drawing, Harris has managed to sustain a varied career, even making a comeback at the age of sixty three with a lighthearted adaptation of Led Zeppelin's rock and roll song *Stairway to Heaven* (1991). Although Harris' chart version did not use the didjeridu, it was used in some recorded and video versions in Australia. Harris' interpretation was just one of twenty four versions of the song recorded as part of a project instigated by Australian television personality Andrew Denton. The song put Harris into the British singles charts and was followed by another chart record in December 1995, *Ergo Sum Pauper (I am a Poor Man)*. The song is accompanied by didjeridu and sung in Latin; accompanied by a Welsh male voice choir and school boys from Eton and backed by a hip hop beat. The song is a cultural synthesis of specialism and marginality. As a specialist instrument the didjeridu accompanies the elitism of Etonians and the unique vocal timbre of Welsh choral voices. Its performance in Latin appropriately combines a marginal language in a synthesis of musical differentiation, through the sounds of four cultures: Aboriginal Australia, Euro-Australia, Wales and Britain.

Aware of the potentialities of the didjeridu, British interest in learning the instrument began in the early 1980s when it was performed at local music festivals. The first 'World Music Village' held in 1983 at Notting Hill, London, offered a forum for experimentation and interaction with indigenous instruments, musics and musicians. Consequently, it has taken about eighty years to transform the instrument from an inanimate object in a museum to a dynamically vibrant one. In 1988 there were only a handful of people playing the didjeridu with serious intent, but by 1995 the sudden increase in the number of players has meant that there are now at least six booklets available on didjeridu technique, videos such as Australian Alastair Black's *A Beginner's Guide* (1995) and a wider pool of teachers available.

Until recently, didjeridus have been imported to Britain from Australia. This is because of the unavailability of Australian woods and also because few Western musicians know how to make a didjeridu in a traditional manner. However, in the winter of 1987, Leeds based musician Ianto Thornber experimented by fashioning a bamboo didjeridu whilst working at Kakadu National Park in the Northern Territory of Australia. Prolonged chiselling finally resulted in a hollow tube of bamboo and eventually he began to make didjeridu-like sounds. In the same year, he was introduced to David Kanari, a local Aborigine who advised him on how to create a bell end at the bottom and put a mouth piece on it. In Darwin he was later to discover that it was much easier to achieve sounds from a correctly fashioned didjeridu. Back in Britain, he sought to discover easier methods of manufacture and was advised how to hollow out the trunk and plane the edges. This led to the production of his own didjeridus which he expanded into a retail outlet in Leeds, called Boab Didjeridus, which sells both British and Australian-made didjeridus.

With the influx of didjeridus to the United Kingdom and the home production of both didjeridus from £60 ($120 Australian) upwards and 'kidjeridus' at £7 ($14 Australian) the instrument has become widely accessible. Kidjeridus are short pieces of plastic piping about two feet in length with a smaller body capacity, requiring less air pressure to create a drone and thus, are more suitable for children. Variations on the basic shape of the kidjeridu are also produced in the form of sliding kidjeridus, called 'slidjeridus', also made out of plastic and functioning like a sliding trombone.

Construction and innovation in didjeridu design

In the Northern Territory, Yolngu fashion didjeridus by felling the trunk of various different termite-bored types of eucalyptus wood scattered throughout different ecological terrains: red river gum, stringybark tree, yellow box gumtree, bloodwood and wollybutt. The dead trunk is cut to between 1.3–1.5 metres long and any debris inside is hollowed out. The body is further pared to remove the rough bark to make it lighter to carry and to improve the sound quality. Today, British-made didjeridus are fashioned from a number of different hard wood trees; ash, beech, cherry, cotoneaster, lilac, oak and walnut. These construction materials inevitably have an effect on the timbre of the instruments.

Didjeridus produced by Yolngu are painted and named according to the pitch of the fundamental, associated with a song subject which is related to that pitch and the contours of the instrument's body.[3] So, for example, a high pitched didjeridu may be named after a spirit because its high drone imitates the sound of the spirit's call in the forest. Another didjeridu might be called *Wititj*, 'Olive Python', as 'the twisted trunk of the tree was said to resemble the snake's body and because its deep resonant pitch was imitative of its ritual sound in the thunder' (Magowan 1994: 283). Didjeridus imported from this region are painted with ritual designs, although they may depict 'outside' or 'less restricted' representations of an ancestral journey.[4] When men decorate didjeridus for commercial sale they may leave out some of the artistic details of their clan's ancestral story. Although it is highly unlikely that Westerners would realise this to be the case, these omissions provide a means of protecting levels of sacred clan knowledge and the authority of elders who hold the right to restrict aspects of that knowledge from women and children. While the designs will look slightly different, (perhaps by depicting fewer animals, or by illustrating less intricate geometric patterns), masking details does not destroy the original sacredness of the design, it merely covers up certain elements of the power of the total ancestral event.

Because few Western artists who paint didjeridus understand the complexity of meanings in traditional ritual designs, they have adapted and combined a mixture of artistic styles. For example, some of Boab Didjeridus' instruments produced by Thornber have been painted in the dot art style characteristic of Central Australia. However, Thornber's Western artwork was not wholly inspired by the techniques and styles of the Centre but also from the notion of 'viral evolution' in computer programming. Some of these didjeridus were painted with orange and red dots spiralling inwards and outwards creating a series of circles coming together until they met. The designs were generated from the idea that computer viruses try to expand but are eventually unable to go any further.

The didjeridu in its ritual context

Throughout the Arnhem Land region of the Northern Territory, the didjeridu is used in a variety of ritual contexts: for commemorative and memorial purposes, initiation, circumcision and death. The songs performed by each group must be accompanied by *one* didjeridu player while the songmen beat clapsticks.[5] It is unthinkable that two didjeridu players should perform together or that musicians should play as a group. Men also never play purely for listening purposes or entertainment. However, young boys are allowed to play 'fun' songs when they are learning the patterns of the didjeridu.[6]

The performance of the didjeridu in a ritual context is part of a system of reciprocal obligation. Singers belong to clans that stand in specific kinship relations to each other. The clans are comprised of patrilineages. From birth, an individual automatically acquires his or her identity patrilineally, giving him or her access to ritual knowledge and action. In addition, he or she can draw upon matrilineal connections to establish rights to land, rights in women or in the manufacture of ritual objects, or call upon members of their mother's clan to help perform songs and dances. Thus, in a ritual context, sister's sons of one moiety (a half of the social whole) will play the didjeridu for the opposite moiety and vice versa. However, women are not taught to play the didjeridu because of its sacred role in performance and its metaphorical connections with ancestral symbols that are male oriented.[7]

The role of the didjeridu in Yolngu ritual then, is to support the singers and dancers. Musicians aim to create an atmosphere conducive to a virtuosic performance through sharply articulated rhythms, dynamic punctuations of calls and the insertion of the overtone (usually between a tenth and a twelfth above the fundamental). Thus, the didjeridu is an integral part of the entire musical event. Didjeridu rhythms provide timed guidelines for the intricate elaboration of men and women's basic steps. The faster rhythms enable men to add accentuated stamps in their footwork, while women make smaller, more rapid movements with their knees bent, flicking sand over each foot and moving the raised foot back and forth in succession. Without the patterned rhythms of the didjeridu, the song words would lack articulation to a metrical pulse and the agile and controlled foot movements of the dancers also would be lost.

Void of this entire ritual system, Western musicians in Great Britain and Ireland choose to play for their own entertainment as soloists and in bands, combining

Western instruments with the didjeridu to achieve exotic sounds in a popular music medium. However, in an attempt to create new musical sounds, and with the increasing numbers of performers, the didjeridu is not often recorded as a solo instrument. The most recent experimentation with the didjeridu is to form didjeridu orchestras. These groups play at didjeridu workshops and larger festivals. They involve multiple musicians, with sometimes seventy or eighty didjeridus sounding simultaneously. Didjeridu gatherings reached an apex in September 1992 at the Glastonbury Festival when an (alleged) world record number of two hundred fifty two didjeridus performed together. The event was organised by didjeridu player Cyrung from the group Tribal Drift. The didjeridus were arranged into common groups of fundamentals, each section playing their own rhythms which created a wave of sound surging across the stage.

The concept behind didjeridu orchestras appears to be the more players the better and the greater the sound, the more intense the experience. This generates a clear dichotomy with Yolngu principles of practice where the clarity and precision of one didjeridu is of paramount importance. It is a nonsense to Yolngu to think of duet or orchestral didjeridu groups as this would mar the brilliance and intensity of an individual performer's sound.

Ritual context

Thus far I have not addressed how authentic Aboriginal didjeridu music might be defined, as it presents a complex of possible positions. In general, however, the majority of didjeridu music is performed in a ritual context and it is the rhythmic patterns accompanying ritual songs which are considered to be traditional. Non-Aboriginal musicians are aware that the didjeridu comprises an integral part of Aboriginal ritual, where Aborigines are accountable to ideal notions of ancestral performance animated by ancestral power. This is where authenticity becomes problematic for non-Aboriginal performers. There is an inherent contradiction in their desire to recreate 'primordial' sounds akin to the musical ideals of Aboriginal performers and the knowledge that they cannot do so in the same way, since Aborigines regard themselves as spiritual vessels for the reinstatement of their ancestral past. If authenticity in Aboriginal music is taken to be consensus on the manifestation of that which always has been from time immemorial, its realisation is dependent upon the receptivity of the performer to her or his ancestral origins. In this respect, what constitutes authentic Aboriginal music is measured in relation to a performer's skill, knowledge, power and ability to open the essence of the ancestral inside to the world outside. Aboriginal performance then, is always under scrutiny even within their own system since different clans will have particular expectations with regard to pitch, timbre, rhythm and the rhythmic relationship with the singer.

Unlike the schools of classically trained musicians in Britain who aim to learn instrumental techniques in the styles of various composers and periods of Western music history, all the didjeridu performers that I spoke to asserted that they were not trying to copy Aboriginal performance per se, an act that they considered cultural plagiarism. Instead, they asserted they were trying to capture the spiritual ambience and atmosphere behind it. However, by avoiding recourse to Aboriginal technical or rhythmical style, Western musicians are confronted with a double bind. As long as they refrain from using Aboriginal rhythms it would appear the spiritual ambience is denied them also, since the appropriation of authentic didjeridu music can only be achieved through the performance of ritual didjeridu rhythms. By avoiding Aboriginal rhythms, British performers ensure they do not create a stereotype of Aboriginal didjeridu performance, nor do they adopt the ritual seniority associated with skilled performance and they do not make themselves accountable to ideals of authentication in a contested area of ritual performance.

The most common context for Yolngu music-making is at funerals. Four or five clans stand in a close relationship to the deceased and are required to sing the deceased back to the land of the dead. Everything in the Yolngu world, including people and spirits, belongs to one of two moieties, called *Dhuwa* and *Yirritja*. When Yolngu die they have a soul and a spirit named *birimbirr* and *mokuy* which must be returned to one of two sacred areas. Deceased Dhuwa members return to Burralku, an island off the coast and Yirritja members return to *Milnguya*, the 'Milky Way'.

The didjeridu accompanies the funerary songs which tell of the ancestral journeys of 'spirit beings' who crossed the land and created sacred sites in the landscape in the distant past. For example, crocodiles gouged out rivers, their heads became rocky cliff formations and their eyes the round freshwater holes in clearings near the coast. They stopped at several places on the way and left clans at each site before continuing on. At last, each ancestor's journey was over and they went inside the ground depositing their spiritual power. In every ritual context, the spiritual significance of musical and dramatic action is of paramount importance. The act of singing imbues the participants with the power to imagine the movements of the soul on its way, while dancing embodies spiritual power to affect its journey.

Thus, it is crucial that the correct songs of each clan are performed at each place. If one element of the music is absent, if the song words are inappropriate, or if the song is inaccurately or carelessly executed then the performance will, at best be ineffective and at worst, be in danger of angering the *mokuy* spirit of the deceased. The *mokuy* will be left behind to trouble family relatives and cause sickness. It is, in part, the power of the words and their ability to evoke impressive images that transport the soul of the deceased to its resting place. However, in order to be effective, they must be animated by the complexities of the rhythmic accompaniment. Thus, the drone of the didjeridu and its capacity for intricate

167

rhythmic variations, are fundamental in creating a dynamic arena for the interplay of speech, sound and spiritual invocation.

If British artists are not playing the didjeridu as part of a ritual event, it is questionable whether there is any spiritual appeal at all. It is evident that some bands use the didjeridu to evoke spirituality more overtly than others and that some will experience a heightened effect of transcendence or physical alteration of some kind, perhaps as a physiological result of circular breathing. This has been assessed in various ways. Steve Boakes, didjeridu player for the Levellers has commented ambivalently that:

> *I think it has a spiritual effect. After playing for some time I feel light headed, but that's due to oxygenation. Sometimes it can be very hypnotic and put you into a trance-like mentality and other times it can bore you silly.* (unattributed, nd)[8]

However, the didjeridu is finding its spiritual niche in Britain. Edinburgh University's Centre for Continuing Education is offering evening courses in Shamanism which aim to allow people to 'experience at first-hand the beauty and mystery of the spiritual domain'.[9] Originating in New York and inspired by anthropological studies from the Americas, Polynesia and India, shamanic workshops have sprung up across the world. The Edinburgh group practices neo-shamanic journeying through tunnels to shamanic states of consciousness accompanied by the monotonous booming of the didjeridu as well as drums and rattles (Willis, 1994: 16). In these states participants envisage powerful animals, psychedelic colours and scenes from previous eras, indicative of a divided ego-awareness which the practitioners are concerned to enhance.

The didjeridu and music therapy

When the didjeridu is used as part of New Age spirituality and neo-shamanism, it is involved in the creation of meditative states which also overlap with the use of the didjeridu in alternative therapies. Some alternative healers use the didjeridu for breathing, dances, hypnosis and music meditation to affect the physical, psychological and psychosomatic state of the patient. Strobel (cited in Schellberg, 1993) reports incidences where patients reported experiencing images of themselves either interacting with, or transforming into, animals or other states, conjured up by didjeridu sounds. He relates that the images evoked include powerful, wild animals such as buffalo, elephants and tigers as well as a panorama of landscapes from bubbling lava inside the earth to the vast desert expanses. Women have reported being transported into feelings of pregnancy or even going through labour and birth (70–71). Strobel also notes that some therapists consider that these hallucinations are experienced because the sound of the didjeridu is akin to the sounds produced inside the womb. (ibid)

For a while, Farrenden worked in conjunction with an alternative therapist who focused on Eastern methods of healing. In healing sessions the harmonics of the didjeridu are said to balance the *chakras*, the sensitive points within the body.

> *There are seven main Chakras along the spinal column. In order to treat a patient the therapist will play over the patient's body. If one of the Chakras is not active or only partially active the health of the person is affected. Playing over the Chakras can open them up.* (Schellberg, 1993: 63–64)

The sounds of the didjeridu are purported also to affect chakras that intersect with acupuncture or meridian points identified in Chinese medicine. These meridians further react in response to the didjeridu by activating *chi*, energy from outside and transferring it inside the body. These effects take place as the patient hears the sounds of the throbbing fundamental. The same effect also can be felt by didjeridu players. According to Diamond (cited in Schellberg, 1993), this is because 'One of the meridian channels ends in the lips which can be constantly stimulated by vibrations of the didjeridu' (62).

The images of therapeutic experiences are inherent in the titles of Farrenden's pieces, *Dance for an Enchanted Land, Birth of the First Day* and *Serpents Entwine* and in the nature of their sounds. The notion of serpents entwining could be read in two ways. It could be considered to be associated with the chakras which are sometimes represented as spirals entering the body at certain spots, or it could be an embodiment of Australian Aboriginal power. The cassette cover cleverly combines the images of Australia, its land, its ancestral creator and the sunset, with Western concepts of the same symbols. The front collage of turtles, vine leaves, the desert and the sunset is depicted in dot design characteristic of Central Australia, while the inside cover uses the cross-hatching of Yolngu painting. Hence, the cover mirrors the fusion of ideologies heard in the music. Today Farrenden's geographic emphasis is shifting as he is currently focusing on combining a meditative use of didjeridu sounds with African and North American First Nations' drum sounds.

British groups that use the didjeridu are not only appealing to an ideology of New Age, therapy and meditation but also to a fusion of global identities leaning towards a politics of social justice. The 1995 recording *Fundamental* combines themes of intolerance towards racial oppression and cultural paternalism within an ethos of striving for global peace and love. Although these themes may resonate with the context of song texts of popular Aboriginal music, *Fundamental* comprises an eclectic mixture of instrumental and musical influences from New Zealand, Australia, Islam, India and Africa. Its philosophy is expressed in its sleeve notes, which state that: 'Countless other instruments have been used by mankind from day one as a carrier for information, propaganda, story-telling enlightenment, communicating with our chosen Gods and entertainment'.

Fundamental brings together a wide variety of these instruments, creating a blend of cultural musical fusion. It stands, perhaps, at an extreme pole of hybridity generating unique contours of a global music chaos which appears to transcend, if not detach itself from any association with authenticity. In the fusion of musics it would seem that recordings such as *Fundamental* are attempting to challenge the dominant propagation of State and Nationhood. The kaleidoscope of musics generate a 'spontaneous collective identity and a personally felt patriotism' (Frith, 1987: 141). As nations continue to define themselves within broad notions of cultural identity (of which musical genres are a part), global music fusion presents a singular opposition to cultural separation whilst manifesting its own pluralities. The compositions are an engaging of cultural synthesis whilst retaining a sense of inherent individuality and difference. The reason that pluralism emerges through an effort to create singularity and synthesis is because musicians want 'to feel that they are in touch with an essential part of themselves, their emotions and their community' (Stokes, 1993: 13). Consequently, the national melting pot of *Fundamental* serves to reinforce the absence of a single nationalism but effect a multiple national conscience.

Didjeridu performance in Britain

Shaun Farrenden

Not all British didjeridu players choose to compose music to synthesisers, percussion and guitars. Shaun Farrenden, for example, produced two recordings of didjeridu music comprising a set of solo pieces and a set of duets. One of the keys to successful duet performance is considered to be the intricate interlocking of two rhythms each complementing the other. However, some didjeridu players have criticised the simplicity of some duet playing when one player drones and the other sounds a supporting rhythm. With this recording of duets on the market, Farrenden is one of the more recent contributors to the genre.

Farrenden began learning the didjeridu in 1990, playing with friends at music festivals.[10] His duet recording *Double Spiral* (1992), composed with Justin Chester, centres around long sections of continuous didjeridu rhythms which are punctuated by occasional motifs, such as barking into the didjeridu, adding clapstick beats or slightly increasing the tempo.[11] The rhythms are notably Western in style, with the staccato rhythms and shouts of Yolngu didjeridu accompaniments being absent. Farrenden places an emphasis on producing a vast range of swirling sounds by manipulating the embouchure in a consistent rhythm. Tonal variation is developed very gradually, always within a regular pattern. His repeated patterns with only minute changes, are reminiscent of minimalist music, creating a regularity that is hypnotic in effect. In order to achieve a meditative

170

state, the pieces are considerably longer than the average duration of Yolngu didjeridu song accompaniments which usually last one to two minutes. His music relies on expanding the timbre of the didjeridu, allowing the fundamental to broaden, resonate and echo before retracting the sound to a focused hard single tone. This technique is repeated over and over again within the same piece.[12] It is this expansion and contraction of the timbre which is singular to Farrenden's didjeridu style and these elements are a common feature of New Age music.

The didjeridu is becoming increasingly popular with Travellers and New Age followers because its sound has been culturally appropriated to values of 'wholeness, spirituality, relationships, self-healing, universal brotherhood and sisterhood, creativity and oneness with the universe' (Regeneri, 1993: 23). It is considered that the continuous and monotonous drone of the didjeridu can transcend consciousness and move the listener or performer from a mundane to a liminal state. Therefore the instrument is an ideal candidate for New Age music (characterised by repetition and minute variation), as the aim is to realise the indeterminacy of the moment. In addition, New Age music fuses styles, techniques and genres to generate a new type of music. The range of sounds produced on the didjeridu are also able to be manipulated in varying musical contexts, thereby blurring the distinctions between musical genres. Consequently, the didjeridu acts upon a sound space to transform it and recreate it as well as those who participate in that space. Hall (1994) has argued that New Age embodies 'a self conscious experience of the indeterminate, the decentered and the transitional' (13). So it could be considered that the didjeridu has been absorbed by New Age music, through artists such as Farrenden, as it easily blends its shifting frequencies to alter the flow of consciousness.

Cyrung

Like Farrenden, other players, such as Cyrung, are keen to show that the didjeridu is an instrument that can affect mood and emotion. Apart from organising didjeridu orchestras, Cyrung has produced a recording called *Spirit People* (1990) which uses nine didjeridus and acoustic percussion. His music is inspired by the rhythms and sounds of nature, layering the timbres and pitches of mass didjeridu playing with interjections of shouts and calls reminiscent of lions in the jungle and birds in the trees.[13] He also aims to transform states of mind by entering into the 'spirit' of the sounds. However, his additional reliance on drum rhythms and multiple didjeridus accentuates the range of timbres. The thickly layered texturing produces a gamut of intertwined patterns and its overall effect is akin to New Age recordings that reproduce sounds of nature e.g. Gibson's *Solitudes: Exploring Nature with Music* (1993). In both tracks on Side Two of *Spirit People*, *Jungle* and *Life*, Cyrung combines a melee of didjeridu sounds with dynamic African drum rhythms to add to their mysterious rustic tonal colours. As Cyrung does not use any electronic effects, his music has a raw

171

natural sound generated by the original timbre of the instruments. While both Farrenden and Cyrung aim to move people, their soundscapes do not carry the multiplicity of connotations inherent in a Yolngu ritual context.

Ianto Thornber

Another British didjeridu player whose music is influenced by that of other cultures is Ianto Thornber. Like Farrenden, Thornber aims to create a mesmerising music, but one that is further away from traditional sounds of the didjeridu related to nature. It is an approximation to the rock music world, combining the didjeridu with acoustic and electronic experiments in vocals and keyboards. His style has been influenced largely by Stephen Kent, who released the recordings *Somewhere* and *Songs from the Burnt Earth* in 1992 and *The Event Horizon* and *Trance Mission* in 1993.[14] Inspired by Kent's style, he produced a recording in 1990 entitled *Bush Giants* recorded with Anita Hurst, Simon Sanders and Phillip Pinnock.

Thornber's style also focuses on shifting tone qualities through subtle manipulations of the lips, mouth and tongue, exploring an infinite variety of spaces and sounds. In his musical approach, the total soundscape is as important as being able to isolate rhythms and timbres. The two elements, computer music and the didjeridu proved a strong attraction to achieve interesting soundscapes since as a non-musician, he could still create the musical effects he desired. Although the didjeridu requires practise and control it does not demand reading musical scores, just as it requires minimal technical keyboard expertise to play previously sampled sounds from the computer. As sounds are emphasised, the intricacy of rhythms are of secondary importance. The only piece on the recording that was initially composed around didjeridu rhythms is *Capoeira*. Its musical shape is derived from Brazilian samba lines. To achieve a wide range of sounds all the other songs were composed by first laying down sampled sounds on computer and then playing them on the keyboard, only the vocal and didjeridu parts were played live.

The range of sounds is enhanced by Thornber's integration of different didjeridus for different effects. For example, on a short, loud didjeridu with a wide aperture the didjeridu produces rasping sounds. In the piece *Berserker* Thornber uses a didjeridu with a high fundamental (F) to achieve these coarser, harsher sounds as the music works itself into the frenzy the title suggests. For more mellow sounds he chooses didjeridus in E-flat. Thornber commonly plays didjeridus in C, C-sharp, D, E and E-flat.[15] The result of the music on the recording is a mixture of synthesised noises with explosive screams and twisting timbres. His philosophy is to create an organic musical core of kaleidoscopic sounds. He has commented that 'my idea of playing the didjeridu is to get lost in swirls in the mind whilst having an evocative drum beat that complements the rhythm of the heartbeat'.[16] While Thornber plays to explore the scope of the didjeridu he does not claim to affect healing. However, as new sounds emerge and the instrument is stretched far beyond its indigenous usage, many Westerners have claimed therapeutic benefits, or physiological and psychological transformation of some degree. But, unlike Yolngu, Westerners do not play the didjeridu within a ritual context to articulate systematically with the spiritual realm.

Graeme Wiggins

If Thornber represents one style along a spectrum, positioned at considerable distance from traditional Yolngu performance practice, it is possible that there are artists who might consciously adopt certain aspects of Yolngu musical style and thus, approach some idea of 'authenticity' in didjeridu playing. However, there are few who fit this category. Only a handful of British musicians have had prolonged stays in any Aboriginal community and even if they have, they often do not attempt to imitate the patterns of Aboriginal song accompaniments. This lack of first-hand experience with the indigenous use of the didjeridu has had resonances in all aspects of Western didjeridu performance, in terms of group formations, musical genres, didjeridu styles and their surrounding philosophies. To date, only one performer has produced commercial music with traditional Yolngu didjeridu patterns.

Graham Wiggins began playing the didjeridu in 1982. Two recordings were initially released with his group Outback which was formed in 1988. These combined dance rhythms on the didjeridu with drums and guitar solos. As an undergraduate student he completed a thesis on the physics of the didjeridu at Boston College and later, a Ph.D. in Physics at Oxford University. This led him to develop the world's first keyed didjeridu, a complex instrument that is a cross between a didjeridu and a saxophone. The keys allowed a range of notes to sound instead of a single drone.[17] In 1992, Wiggins spent some time on Elcho Island in the Northern Territory learning traditional Yolngu rhythms. Although his performance style could be considered to be playing with Yolngu rhythms, he did not expressly try to imitate Yolngu patterns until 1994, with the release of his recording *Dr. Didg Out of the Woods*.

Brolga is the one didjeridu piece that fuses Yolngu ritual music with Wiggins' own didjeridu style. The piece begins with a recording of the original song made in 1992 with Litalita Ganambarr singing and Dhakalin Burarrwanga on the didjeridu. After several repetitions of the theme, Wiggins takes over the didjeridu accompaniment in exact imitation of Dhakalin. The guitars then develop the tune before the music returns to the original recording. Consistency with Yolngu style is evidenced in this recording in the regular patterning of the didjeridu accompaniment within each song verse.[18] As in ritual songs, the *Brolga* song becomes more agitated as the piece progresses, with motivic development in the guitar and didjeridu. In Yolngu songs the gradual increases in the tempo of the song accompaniment image a change in action of the animal, bird, element or ancestor.

Graeme Wiggins (1995).

For example, in the song of the Dhuwa salt water, *gapu monuk*, the didjeridu tempo is slow and the song words tell that the sea is calm. As the wind grows stronger, stirring up the waves it eventually causes white-caps to break and the tempo of the didjeridu accelerates with additional tongued patterns and more frequent interjections of the overtone. This progression, from slow droning, with few overtone articulations, to faster patterns with rapid tonguing, is featured at some point in the majority of clan song subjects.

In addition, the didjeridu player will tap out syncopated rhythms to the singing, or the accompanying rhythm of the men's clapstick beat on the body of the didjeridu with a finger or a stick. When the song is finished the didjeridu always terminates with a tell-tale alternation from the fundamental to the overtone and back again. This occurs before the singer concludes the song, generally with a descending vocal coda. In Wiggins' composition, the return to the original Yolngu *Brolga* song, dying away after several repetitions, could be thought of as analogous to the descending vocal coda when the last singer repeats some of the text to conclude the song.

Wiggins' music is influenced specifically by the northeast Arnhem Land didjeridu traditions but it should be noted that musical stylistics vary in the northwest of the region. The latter have a relatively wide melodic range of an octave or more. Unlike songs in the northeast, the songs in this region always end with the didjeridu or clapsticks after the voice has finished (Moyle, 1974: 38–39). The clapstick accompaniments are not necessarily unison beats and this will affect the didjeridu player if he taps out a rhythm on the side of the instrument.

Although *Brolga* is an ingenious attempt to build on Yolngu rhythms and song, it raises the question of the sacredness of the song and its suitability for other performance contexts. As all didjeridu rhythms accompany the sacred texts of Yolngu song, the patterns themselves are an innate part of the spiritual power of the piece. Extracting the music from its ritual context raises problems over the desecration of sacred material and the violation of rights over the ownership and performance of sacred texts. While it is possible to minimise an outcry over these issues, it is unlikely that all who share rights in the material will be totally contented with the process of adaptation. Wiggins was careful to ensure the owner's permission to use the material and to address issues of copyright and royalties for the performance of the music. However, the process of remuneration is extremely complex in Aboriginal societies. There may be one clan who claims primary ownership to the song material but there will be several other clans who also share rights in performing. Thus, the issue of who gets royalties becomes a matter of negotiation and dispute.

Wiggins' other pieces all reflect his concern as a (self-declared) 'classical jazz pianist' and embody influences ranging from rock n' roll groups such as the Grateful Dead to Afro-Cuban jazz. These influences are further captured in the titles of the other items on the *Dr. Didg Out of the Woods* recording, e.g. *Street Music, Easy, Under the Influence* and *Rave On*. There is little evidence of any appropriation of Yolngu images of kangaroos or sunsets here. In fact, pieces such as *Rave On* are based on heavy metal sounds and *Under the Influence* is explicitly a jazz-funk piece.

Wiggins' performance emphasis is largely on a dance beat and the importance of controlling rhythm with the breath. As he has stated,

> *Playing the didjeridu does not simply use the breath, it is the breath. It is a way of dancing with your lungs and throat and breathing rhythmically to create a hypnotic groove which comes straight from the rhythms of the body.* (i/v)

This dance technique is enhanced by his focus on live sampling, a process of building sounds through a digital delay. A rhythm is sampled onto a continuous loop while another rhythm is then performed on top, sampled and so on. This technique expands the field of sound, rhythm and colour. He has developed this procedure to enable a larger number of sample tracks to play simultaneously, enabling musicians to improvise live whilst incorporating a large a number of variations as possible.

Shozo

Another performer whose technique has some resemblances to Yolngu musical style is that of Shozo. His most recent recording, *Sounds of Breath*, released on the British market in October 1995 on CD, is an extended version of a cassette released in June 1995, entitled *Dobolo Dobolo Music of Breath*. The first cassette was an initial experiment to bridge the gap between electronic manipulations of didjeridu music and aspects of Aboriginal styles of playing. Shozo's pieces are original, yet he acknowledges his debt to both Euro-Australian and Yolngu performers such as Wallis Buchanan (with Jamiroquai) Phillip Conyngham, Alan Dargin, David Hudson, and Gurrumul and Makuma Yunupingu and Milkayngu Munungurr (with Yothu Yindi).

His recording *Sounds of Breath*, includes two new songs, *Simple Tune* and *Journey's End* which are not on the original cassette. In all the pieces Shozo plays solo didjeridu with very clearly articulated didjeridu motifs and with a strong, clear use of the overtone. Each track tends to allow the music to focus on one instrument at a time while another instrument plays an accompanying role. For example, in the song *Yume-No-Ato*, didjeridu patterns are cleverly fused with African drum rhythms. These drum rhythms imitate the didjeridu riffs and eventually take over to complete the piece. Also, the song *Away from Babylon* and the song *On and On and On and ...* both highlight the acoustic piano and bass guitar respectively. In the latter, the bass guitar is reminiscent of the music of some Yolngu rock groups such as Yothu Yindi where the didjeridu plays an accompanying role to a funky bass line. The songs *On and On and On and ...* and *Sailing* are also notable for the accompanying electric bass, absent from the cassette version.

Yolngu influences can be evidenced in other ways in Shozo's music. *Away from Babylon* is unusual in its slow, step-like chord motion, hovering on the tones of one chord before moving to the next. The didjeridu eventually joins in, playing a slowing droning accompaniment. This technique is used is some of the Yirritja moiety's songs when a keyboard may be played inside a funeral shade to the singing of clan songs outside. In its ritual context, the keyboard accompaniment consists of harmonic chords moving in a steady close progression. Not all of Shozo's songs have connections with the sounds of Aboriginal Australia and the music is intended to produce a variety of meditative sounds through the fusion of musical genres. The song *My Sweet Golborne Road* blends the chant of the Koran in an Islamic temple with the accompaniment of the didjeridu, while other items are a direct comment on the society in which Shozo lives: the song *Traffic Jamming* reflects the sound of a traffic jam in Notting Hill Gate, London. The emphasis of both the cassette and the CD is to faithfully reproduce the sounds of the didjeridu without changing or adding to its tone quality and timbre by transforming the sounds through a mixing deck.

176

The didjeridu in Ireland

Although Shozo and Wiggins have both met Yolngu players, neither decided to try and fuse their talents with Aborigines in live performance. Indeed, it took the discovery of ancient Irish horns to inspire a music project between two Irish musicians, Maria Cullen and Simon O'Dwyer and two Australian musicians, Phillip Conyngham and Alan Dargin. Together they produced a recording using the band name Reconciliation entitled *Two Stories in One* (1993). Bronze Age Irish horns were first collected as museum pieces in 1750 and are almost 3000 years old, dating from approximately 1000–800 B.C. The horns had originally been buried in both southern and northern Ireland to preserve them from invaders. They had not been given a concert platform as no one could produce a note from either of the two mouthpieces, one mouthpiece was at the end of the horn and the other was an oval mouthpiece about six inches along one side of the horn.[19] Eventually, Simon O'Dwyer arranged to have the Bronze Age Irish horns recast in 1988 and first exposed their sounds in traditional Irish music performances.

The horns are fashioned in three sizes. The bass horn, *Dord Iseal* produces a droning sound, the mid-range horn, *Dord Ard* makes a drone and three notes. The high side-blown horn or *Adharc* produces a strong high drone but it also has a two and half octave range. All the horns are demonstrated in different tracks on the recording. County Kerry Irish whistle and bodhran player Maria Cullen became fascinated with the horns. She established Ancient Irish Cultural Promotions, arranging both Irish and Australian tours to promote the instruments. O'Dwyer, like Wiggins, went to Arnhem Land, in 1992, where he met Conyngham and Dargin. They experimented with the sounds of the horns and didjeridu together as circular breathing into the instruments produces similar drones and toots. On the Reconciliation album sleevenotes, Cullen commented:

> *The music that we began to create came about as we were busking together at Circular Quay in Sydney. I would play an Irish rhythm or reel time on the bodhran (the Irish drum) and the other three would improvise, making the sound grow to an amazing crescendo.*

The recording comprises arguably the most advanced integration of two indigenous musical genres. In order to blend the two, it is necessary to understand what is meant by 'traditional' in Irish music and how the didjeridu is readily absorbed into it. O'Dwyer says he plays in a 'traditional Irish style' (cited in Casey, 1994: 23) and this is based on rhythms of reels, jigs, hornpipes, polkas, slides, marches, strathspeys, mazurkas, lancers and scottisches (ibid). Many rhythms played on the didjeridu fit easily into these metres.[20] The acceptance of the didjeridu into Irish music shows the adaptability of traditional forms and an openness to innovation, but changes in traditional music have been ongoing since the 17th and 18th Centuries when new musical forms and instruments were imported.

177

Reconciliation (left–right, Simon O'Dwyer, Alan Dargin, Maria Cullen and Phil Cunningham) (1994).

O'Dwyer therefore draws upon his traditional Irish knowledge when playing, but is also influenced by Aboriginal didjeridu styles. The styles that Dargin plays are adaptations of his Aboriginal song rhythms. He does not play sacred patterns in public, considering that those patterns are fixed for ritual purposes and that Aboriginal players are taught to become experts within a style, not to improvise at random. Hence, the skilful performer will be able to increase the complexity of playing within a given framework.

In several pieces on the recording *Reconciliation: Two Stories in One*, the bodhran lends a distinctively Irish flavour to the combination of Aboriginal and Irish instrumentation e.g. *Reconciliation*, *Kerry Polka* and *Jiggery Didj*. Cathy O'Sullivan's performance on the Irish Brass Stringed harp and vocals in *Bis* is strongly reminiscent of the soundscapes of the Irish folkgroup Clannad. *Jiggery Didj* begins with the didjeridu but soon moves into an Irish folksong. While these three songs have strong Irish elements in the music, two tracks featuring the didjeridu highlight political messages about the culture of Aboriginal Australia. *Don't Wake 'Im* and *Jalopy* are songs dealing with repercussions from mining in the Northern Territory and transport developments in Western Australia.

The group's musical style aims to demonstrate the versatility of each of the instruments. *Lilting Horns* allows the horn players to explore the range of sounds of the three horns, while *Polite Conversation* enables the didjeridu player to demonstrate rhythmic virtuosity in elaborate patterns which are echoed on the Kubing (Bamboo Mouth Harp). *Pony Tail Reel* sets the stage for an impressive display of the timbres and rhythms of the Dord Iseal that resembles some didjeridu patterns. The Dord Iseal adds an element of surprise because it produces harmonics when played in the key of E-flat. O'Dwyer adds a mouthpiece to alter the length of the air column thus raising or lowering the pitch (Casey, 1994: 56). All the tracks have a sense that the music is potentially infinite, spiralling in and out, time and again. This spiralling can be heard in the song *Bis*, *bis* is a Gaelic word meaning spiral and the theme is further developed for the design on the recording's cover. The swirls are the intermingling sounds, but can be associated with the wood of the didjeridu itself. The rings of the didjeridu are like the swirls of sound it creates and like Reconciliation, Graeme Wiggins cleverly developed this idea on his own recording's cover, *Dr. Didj Out of the Woods*. This shows photos of the band members set against computer graphics of different rings from the cross-sections of tree trunks.

Conclusion

What is the future of the didjeridu in Britain and Ireland? Will there be any on-going influence from Aboriginal sources such as those of the Yolngu? Will panpipe music in shopping arcades and restaurants be superseded by the drone of the didjeridu in the pubs, clubs and elevators of the millennium? Is its exoticism to be reduced to a trite familiarity like a performance of *Ave Maria* on panpipes, or is its power of sound and form such that its arenas of acceptable performance are ever-increasing?

The sounds of the didjeridu appeal on several levels and can be read in different cultural contexts and with varying intentions. For example, British neo-shamanic ideology brings didjeridu music closer to panpipe music encapsulating the music of dreams, of escape and of commercial appeal through a romantic exoticism. Its sound effects could be considered akin to elevator music: it goes up and down, swirls in and out, like the elevator loop cassette that plays over and over again, with no beginning and no ending. It is timeless, like the elevator itself, passing between floors without any ultimate destination, yet, every stop is its own destination. Similarly, didjeridu music for healing purposes is hypnotic and repetitive, broken only by accentuation points on the overtone, but still producing an infinite sound.

The artists discussed in this chapter provide us with contrasting styles and approaches to the value and musical capacities of the didjeridu. In Western, as in Yolngu performance, didjeridu players consider that individual styles are readily distinguishable. These styles represent a continuum from Wiggins' attempt to approximate and appropriate Yolngu ritual song patterns into his compositions, following a virtuosic folkstyle based around complex rhythms, to Thornber's exploration of didjeridu sounds to affect mood and sensation.[21]

Some British and Irish players admit they have been influenced by Aboriginal performers but, for the most part, they are not intentionally using their traditional rhythms. While Reconciliation have attempted to retain characteristics from the traditional musics of Ireland and Australia, the result of combining the two cultures is a hybrid blend that takes on its own distinct contours. Yolngu didjeridu stylistics are specifically related to ancestral ideology and performance must be an entire package of ancestral drama animated by song and dance. For British and Irish players this aspect is not a main concern and in terms of the instrument's authenticity, they are playing 'out of time' in two ways. Firstly, in Britain and Ireland didjeridu music comprises isolated, individual pieces. It comprises music of the moment, not pieces reinstated from an ancestral past by spirit beings. Secondly, New Age adherents intend to affect the musical atmosphere by continually altering sounds and rediscovering new sounds. In contrast, in Australia the Yolngu bring the past into the present and take the present into the past as they recreate the sounds of a primordial era, musically recounting ancestral action and event.

Didjeridu performance in Britain and Ireland may also be considered 'out of place' in comparison with its traditional ritual arena. It is clearly devoid of its symbolic and aesthetic ritual role and has entered other performance arenas, including classical, popular, folk and jazz. These contexts are served by a variety of performance spaces: the concert stage, the cellar bar, the rural club, Stonehenge, or pavement busking. Indeed, it would seem anywhere can become a space for the didjeridu in Britain and Ireland, rather than a site-specific ritual ground. Now that the didjeridu has overcome its long-held curiosity status, it remains to be seen whether its application in varying contexts is merely a passing phase, just as the panpipes are heard in the most familiar surrounds of shopping arcades and elevators. Today, music technology has revolutionised accessibility to the raw sounds of the didjeridu. What is certain is that the didjeridu has been brought from the vast expanses of the Australian Outback to the comfort of the hearths of Britain and Ireland with innumerable possibilities for its cultural appropriation and performance.

Acknowledgements: Thanks to Ianto Thornber, Shaun Farrenden and Graham Wiggins who contributed to this piece in interviews and provided music recordings. Thanks also to Hélene La Rue, Alan Marcus, Karl Neuenfeldt and Martin Stokes for their assistance in this research.

Notes

1. Much controversy surrounds the notion of what constitutes 'traditional' in Aboriginal Australia. I employ the term here to refer to indigenous religious belief and its concomitant ritual practices.

2. Personal communication,Hélene La Rue, Pitt Rivers Museum, Oxford, 1994.

3. In one ritual, men sing a number of different topics, or song subjects, that tell of the travels of an ancestral being from place to place and its actions along the way. The entire complement of a group of song subjects is known as a song series. (See Clunies-Ross and Wild, 1988).

4. Keen (1994), Morphy (1991) and Berndt (1974) discuss the relative and changing nature of knowledge that is secret in some contexts and yet can become open knowledge over time.

5. Women sing at moments determined by the men, when the soul has reached its destination each day. They perform in a separate crying-song style, wailing and singing the tunes in long slow lines (Magowan, 1995).

6. Young men have their own song repertoire called *djatpangarri*. These are fun or nonsense songs which teach the boys the rhythms of the didjeridu and help them gain confidence in ritual singing.

7. I knew of only one skilled female performer on the didjeridu during my fieldwork on Galiwin'ku, northeast Arnhemland. She was the daughter of a renowned didjeridu player and had shown aptitude and gained respect for her ability. Although, to my knowledge, she did not perform in any rituals.

8. Unattributed, unpaginated and undated photocopied article entitled 'Steve Boakes and the Levellers' supplied to the author by Ianto Thornber.

9. Course publicity.

10. He still performs in such contexts. At the 1995 Glastonbury Festival he offered 'massages' where he would play the didjeridu over the customer's body, massaging the body with the sound waves, as a 'healing' practice. Personal correspondence with Philip Hayward, 1995.

11. These sounds are evident in *Rainmaker* and *Feeding the Flames*.

12. The technique can be heard in *Cooinda Dreaming*.

13. These sounds can be heard on *Inside Out* (1990).

14. Stephen Kent now lives and works in the San Francisco Bay Area.

15. Thornber has fashioned one didjeridu in A but its seven foot long body makes it considerably more difficult to produce continuous rhythms.

16. Personal Communication, July 1995.

17. This instrument can be heard in *Sun Tan*.

18. Two songs, *Easy* and *Sun Tan* use this technique.

19. Keith Maguire, personal communication to Karl Neuenfeldt.

20. An excellent analysis of the comparison between the rhythms of the didjeridu and Irish music can be found in Casey (1994), especially pages 33–35.

21. The appropriation of Yolngu techniques is problematic, as styles are not homogenous (Knopoff, 1995: 28).

181

Bibliography

Berndt R. (1974) *Australian Aboriginal Religion* Leiden: Brill.

Bos R. (1980) 'Didjeridu Theology', *Nungalinya Occasional Bulletin* n8, July.

Casey C. (1994) 'The Use of the Didjeridu in Irish Traditional Music', (unpublished) M.A. Thesis, Queen's University, Belfast.

Clunies-Ross M. and Wild S. (1988) 'Formal Performance: The relations of Music, Text and Dance in Arnhem Land Clan Songs', *Ethnomusicology*, v28 n2.

Diamond J. (1990) *Lebensenergie in der Musik*, Südergellersen: Verlag Bruno Martin.

Duncan A. (1995) 'No One Ever Knows What I'll Do Next', *The Radio Times* 2–8/12.

Frith S. (1987) 'Towards an Aesthetic of Popular Music' in Leppert R and McClary S (eds) *Music and Society*, Cambridge: Cambridge University Press.

Goehr L. (1992) *The Imaginary Museum of Musical Works*, Oxford: Clarendon Press.

Hall D. (1994) 'New Age Music: A Voice of Liminality in Postmodern Popular Culture', *Popular Music and Society*, v18 n2.

Harris J. (1990) *One Blood: 200 Years of Aboriginal Encounter with Christianity*, Oxford: Lion.

Keen I. (1994) *Knowledge and Secrecy in an Aboriginal Religion*, Oxford: Clarendon Press.

Knopoff S. (1997) 'Accompanying the Dreamtime: Determinants of Didjeridu Style in Traditional and Popular Yolngu Song' (this anthology).

Magowan F. (1994) 'Melodies of Mourning', (unpublished) D. Phil. Thesis, Oxford University.

Magowan F. (1995) 'Songs of the Spirit or Spirit Songs?: Issues of Conflict and Confluence in Australian Aboriginal Music Syncretism', *Manchester Working Papers*, Manchester University.

Morphy H. (1984) *Journey to the Crocodile's Nest*, Canberra: Australian Institute of Aboriginal Studies.

Morphy H. (1991) *Ancestral Connections*, Chicago: University of Chicago Press.

Moyle A. (1974) *Songs from the Northern Territory Companion Booklet*, Canberra: Australian Institute of Aboriginal Studies.

Regeneri D. (1993) 'Lecture on New Age Music' Four Seasons Records, Louisville, Kentucky, cited in Grove Hall, S (1994) 'New Age Music: An Analysis of an Ecstasy', *Popular Music and Society*, v18 n2.

Rudder J. (1977) *Introduction to Yolngu Science*, Galiwin'ku (Australia): Adult Education Service.

Schellberg D. (1993) *Didgeridoo: Ritual Origins and Playing Techniques*, Holland: Binkey Kok.

Sholl A. (1995) 'New Life for a Dead Lingo', *The Australian* 22/12.

Stokes M. (1993) *Ethnicity, Identity and Music*, Oxford: Berg.

Strobel W. (1992) 'Das Didgeridoo und seine Rolle in der Musiktherapie', *Musiktherapeutische Umschau* n13.

Warner L. (1937) *A Black Civilisation*, London: Harper and Row.

Willis R. (1994) 'New Shamanism', *Anthropology Today*, v10 n6.

Discography

Cyrung *Spirit People* Expand Productions, 1990.

Cyrung *Inside Out*, Expand Productions, 1990.

Shaun Farrenden *Double Spiral*, 1992, BNR.

Fundamental *Fundamental* Beggars Banquet, 1995.

David Gibson *Solitudes: Exploring Nature with Music*, David Gibson Productions.

Stephen Kent *Songs from the Burnt Earth*, Burnt Earth Music, 1992.

Reconciliation *Two Stories in One* Natural Symphonies, 1993.

Shozo *Dobolo Dobolo Music of Breath*, Gullwing Studio, 1995.

Shozo *Sounds of Breath,* Gullwing Studio, 1995.

Ianto Thornber *Bush Giants,* Micromagic, 1990.

Graham Wiggins *Dr. Didj Out of the Woods*, Rykomusic, 1994.

Yothu Yindi *Tribal Voice,* Mushroom Records, 1992.

Index

184